Latin

in

American Schools

Teaching the Ancient World

Sally Davis

Wakefield High School and H.B.
Woodlawn Program, Arlington, Virginia

Scholars Press   Atlanta, Georgia

Latin

in

American Schools

Teaching the Ancient World

Sally Davis

©1991
American Philological Association

Library of Congress Cataloging in Publication Data

Davis, Sally, 1938-
  Latin in American schools : teaching the ancient world / Sally
  Davis.
  p. cm.
  Includes bibliographical references.
  ISBN 1-55540-621-1
  1. Latin language—Study and teaching—United States. I. Title.
PA 2065.U5D38 1991
470'.71'073—dc20   91-24960
                                                          CIP

Table of Contents

Preface

The Report on Latin in American Schools is a result of the conference on the Classics in American Schools held at the University of Virginia in September, 1986. It is the outcome of several years of hard work and solid research by a committee chaired by Sally Davis. The report is a significant achievement both for professional teachers of classical subjects and for students and their parents. Ms. Davis and her colleagues have richly earned our gratitude.

Teachers of Latin and other classical subjects have responded positively to the many pressures put upon them in recent years as a result of shifting priorities in American education. They have considered their field within the broader context of American society and its needs in education, and they have attempted to meet the needs and expectations of the community without sacrificing traditionally high academic standards. A primary goal of the present report is to strike the proper balance between these two potentially conflicting needs.

Secondly, classical teachers have recognized the importance of true and continuing collegiality between teachers in schools and universities. Ms. Davis' committee includes teachers from all levels of schools, public and private, and from colleges and universities. The 1986 conference—supported by grants from the National Endowment for the Humanities, a federal grant-making agency—was presided over jointly by the Presidents of the American Philological Association and the Americal Classical League, and its report, *The Classics in American Schools,* was reviewed by a committee of teachers and scholars from all levels of the profession. The current report is remarkable for its constant emphasis upon collegiality, upon the breaking down of professional barriers, and upon the unity of our profession and our professional goals.

Perhaps this is the most important message that Ms. Davis and her colleagues bring to the educational community in 1990. We all have an interest in the best possible training for our children, the nation's future parents and taxpayers. The report challenges us to work together to bring a traditional subject into its proper place in our system of education, and to involve us all, whatever our role in education, in achieving its goal. It lays the foundation for a new evaluation of the way in which we study and teach a subject that must never be allowed to lose its fundamental place in the education of young citizens.

Mark Morford, Past Vice President, Division of Education, APA
University of Virginia
December, 1990

Preface

It is with great pleasure that I welcome the publication of *Latin in American Schools*. Now, at last, teachers of Latin and Greek, like teachers of several modern foreign languages, will have up-to-date national, professional guidelines, and laypeople and parents will have criteria by which to measure their own Classical education or that of their children. Since the previous national guidelines were published in 1924, these new ones are, to say the least, long overdue. But the long hiatus between these and the previous guidelines probably indicates how immense the task is of collating information about teaching practice among all levels of Latin teaching in a country as large and diverse as ours. Sally Davis and her task force, therefore, deserve our deepest gratitude for completing such a daunting task and completing it so well.

Perhaps the most important conclusion of this report is the exhortation to all Classicists, Classics programs, and Classical organizations to cooperate and help each other. A micro-model of such cooperation has been the harmonious collaboration of Sally Davis' Sub-Committee on National Latin Guidelines and the parent committee, the ACL-APA Joint Committee on the Classics in American Education (JCCAE). Teachers from every level, representing the two largest professional organizations for Classicists, the American Classical League (ACL) and the American Philological Association (APA), have looked objectively, with the widest possible view, at our wonderful, time-honored, common enterprise: the teaching of Latin, Greek, and Classical Humanities. There are problems, we see, but also successes, and the future, if we all continue to work together, is very bright.

Ed Phinney, Immediate Past President, ACL, & Chair, JCCAE
University of Massachusetts at Amherst
December, 1990

Chapter One

Introduction

The study of Latin in the United States appears to be moving in interesting new directions as the twentieth century comes to an end. The traditional activities of this most traditional of subjects—teaching the rudiments of Latin vocabulary and grammar in order to read Latin literature—continue in all areas of the country, in both public and private schools and colleges. An important new partner in the Classical enterprise has emerged in lively programs on the elementary and middle school level. Thousands of young students in all types of educational settings are being introduced to Latin study, and the growing demand for Latin on this level must soon strengthen programs at higher levels.

Several new emphases and pedagogical approaches offer promise in maintaining and increasing enrollments on the secondary level. The most important of these are the reading textbooks that emphasize comprehension over the learning of grammar for its own sake; these seem to hold great appeal to today's high school students. We also see a more widespread and serious teaching of Roman culture and mythology and a strong emphasis on English word study through Latin. In addition to these in-class endeavors, the activities of the Junior Classical League continue to challenge and attract great numbers of American high school students.

On the college level, many changes have taken place in the past several decades—important changes, and some would say unbelievable changes. Greek and Latin majors continue to pursue their studies and many go on to graduate schools for further study. But we now also see the rise of popular courses such as Greek and Roman civilization, mythology, etymology and Classics courses in translation. College Classics departments now teach great numbers of American college students who do not wish to study the ancient languages, but who seek other benefits from Classical studies. Many college students also choose Latin classes to fulfill a two- or four-semester language requirement. College departments that have structured the pace and materials of these introductory courses especially for this category of students have generally shown substantial increase in enrollments.

Yet, while much has changed, one fact remains constant—the heart of any successful Latin program is the teacher. Good teachers bring Latin alive, involve students actively in learning and ultimately change the lives of their students for the better. The fact that Latin continues to show steady and healthy growth is due in large part to the high caliber and special dedication of Latin teachers, who in recent years have fought determinedly for a place in the American curriculum to bring a traditional and difficult subject to modern students. The single most important challenge to our profession today is to produce enough teachers to meet the rising demand of students, parents and administrators for first-rate Latin programs.

The Classical Investigation of 1924

Sixty-nine years ago a veritable task force of prominent American Classicists, sponsored by the General Education Board and the American Classical League, embarked upon The Classical Investigation, a four-year project "for the purpose of ascertaining the present status of Latin and Greek and of preparing a constructive programme of recommendations for improving the teaching of Latin and Greek in the secondary schools of the United States." Clearly, these investigators were acting out of a sense of responsibility to the 940,000 pupils enrolled at that time in secondary Latin courses and the 50,000 in college programs, and out of serious concern for the future of their own profession. The story of what subsequently happened to the teaching of Latin in the United States surely ranks as one of the most striking occurrences in the course of foreign language study during this century in the United States.

Latin Almost Disappears From the Curriculum

The shocking decline of enrollments of Latin in the 1960's and 1970's (from 702,000 students in 1962 to 150,000 in 1976) is not easily or simply explained, but is eminently worthy of study by our profession whose very existence then seemed in doubt. Several important reasons for the crisis are put forth by Professor Ed Phinney in the *Classical Outlook* (66 (1989) 117-25): a new emphasis in the 1960's on science, mathematics and modern languages; the abandonment of Latin by the Roman Catholic Church; and the disillusionment with traditional education as a result of the Vietnam War years. Somehow, a subject that had been considered for more than a century a staple in the general education of very large numbers of American high school students (more than 50% of all high school students in the 1930's) was suddenly considered irrelevant.

The Profession Responds

At that time of crisis many classicists responded by experimenting with new methods and materials of teaching Latin that de-emphasized the traditional grammar-translation method, and made use of inductive strategies, rapid reading approaches and/or the direct method. Classicists also came together in their national and regional associations to initiate heroic efforts to speak out for Latin to administrators, teachers and curriculum supervisors, and to address local, state and federal bodies. As an example, the Classical Association of the Middle West and South (CAMWS) established its Committee for the Promotion of Latin, which, through its thirty-two geographically scattered Vice Presidents, has undertaken numerous kinds of promotional efforts, including advertising, lobbying, providing funds, placing teachers, coordinating newsletters and in general encouraging its entire membership. The success of such efforts as these has encouraged all associations, whether large or small, to expend some of their energy on bringing the merit of their cause to the public eye.

Collaborative Efforts

Besides our regional associations, the American Philological Association (APA) and the American Classical League (ACL) on the national level, and the National Endowment for the Humanities (NEH) on the federal level have contributed to the effort to preserve Classics and Latin. As a result of collaboration among these three powerful bodies, a conference on the teaching of the ancient world was held in 1986 at the University of Virginia. Out of this conference emerged a report, entitled *The Classics in American Schools*, which considers the place of Classics in a democratic system of education and in the American curriculum in general. It has been widely distributed throughout the United States and has served as a handbook for various groups (citizens, parents, administrators and teachers) to initiate, maintain and provide a rationale for the classical content in the school curriculum.

Current Indications of Growth

When we examine the status of present Latin studies, we see many signs that can be considered encouraging. Enrollments have been slowly and steadily rising since the low point of 1976; a profusion of new materials for teaching on all levels continues to appear; diverse and exciting elementary- and middle-school programs are reported from all over the country. The return to traditional educational values, the emphasis on the development of basic writing skills, and the research showing the correlation between Latin study and higher verbal scores on national standardized tests have contributed to the growth of Latin programs everywhere.

Chapter Two

Purpose of the Report and Methodology

The Teaching of Latin in American Schools

This report by the Sub-Committee on National Latin Guidelines (NLG) of the ACL-APA Joint Committee on the Classics in American Education (JCCAE) is an outgrowth of the joint efforts of the APA, ACL and NEH that resulted in the University of Virginia conference and its report, *The Classics in American Schools*. Its purpose is to look specifically at the teaching of Latin in the United States— the healthy developments as well as the problem areas. Further, the NLG sub-committee hopes to offer encouragement and suggestions to teachers, and to provide a set of general curricular guidelines for the teaching of Latin. This report, along with the recommended guidelines, will give all readers an idea of what is happening in Latin studies today, as well as provide teachers and laypeople with a point of reference and a general set of standards for comparison. Another consideration of the JCCAE in the commissioning of this report was the fact that such a broad investigation had not been undertaken since 1924. In light of the current rapidly changing patterns in Latin studies, the ACL and the APA consider the production of this report at this time to be essential for the continued well-being of the profession.

The Sub-Committee on National Latin Guidelines

The Sub-Committee on National Latin Guidelines responsible for this report was appointed by the ACL-APA Joint Committee on the Classics in American Education (JCCAE), which in turn is a standing committee of both the APA and the ACL. The five members of the sub-committee represent expertise and viewpoints that cover the full spectrum of current Latin teaching activities. Sally Davis, chair of the sub-committee and author of this report, has taught high-school Latin for twenty years (and recently middle-school Latin) and works with the ACL/NJCL National Latin Exam and the College Board's Advanced Placement Examinations. Hughlings Himwich is a teacher of Latin, Levels I-V, at Flint School in Fairfax, Virginia, and a State Junior Classical League (JCL) Chair. Bernice Jefferis teaches Classics and Introductory Latin at the Coventry Communications Magnet School in Cleveland Heights, Ohio; she was a fellow of the NEH Aeneid Institute and currently serves as President of the Elementary Teachers of Classics (ETC). Sheila Dickison is an Associate Professor of Classics and an Associate Dean of the College of Arts and Sciences at the University of Florida, Gainesville; she currently serves as Chief Reader of the Advanced Placement Latin Examinations and as a member of the core committee that developed the Florida state certification examination for Latin teachers. Judith Sebesta is a Professor of Classics at the

University of South Dakota, Vermillion, and has worked extensively, as Chair of the ACL Committee on Methodology, to provide programs, workshops and materials for high school and college teachers of Latin.

The *ex officio* members of the committee are Mark Morford, Professor of Classics at the University of Virginia and former Vice-President for Education of the APA, and Ed Phinney, Professor of Classics at the University of Massachusetts at Amherst, Immediate Past President of the ACL and current Chair of the JCCAE. Both of them have offered invaluable advice at every step of the investigation.

The Gathering of Data for the Report

The information presented in this report is based on a number of hearings and panel discussions held by the members of the committee over the last two years in all parts of the country; on a nationwide survey of more than 1200 Latin teachers at all levels; and four follow-up surveys at the different levels. This information has provided the basis for the conclusions and recommendations that follow in this report; however, a brief look at some of the raw data will interest many readers.

Survey Results: Selected Items

The following statistics seem salient. They are not offered as integral parts of a complete picture, but rather as discrete points for separate consideration.

- When asked to rate the reasons why their students had elected to study Latin, 82% of public high school teachers replied that the most important reason to students was to boost their Scholastic Aptitude Test (SAT) scores.

- Only 33% of the teachers thought that the reading of Latin literature in the original language was a very important reason to students for studying Latin.

- Public high school teachers also reported that only 35% of their students spend as much as 30 minutes or more preparing for class.

- Roughly 35% of all secondary-level teachers reported that they do not teach the relative pronoun or the passive voice in the first year.

- Of those teachers who offer an Advanced Placement course, 45% do so after Latin III, 30% after Latin IV and 25% after Latin II.

- The ACL/NJCL National Latin Exam syllabus was an important factor in determining the curriculum of 63% of the respondents, whereas 42% said their state curriculum guide had no influence at all.

- Of the 1226 teachers who responded at all levels, 70% stated that they have other teaching/administrative responsibilities in addition to Latin.

The discussions, recommendations and guidelines in this report are based on the total array of statistical and anecdotal results from the surveys. Teachers' replies to the surveys included many positive comments and suggestions, but also many expressions of uncertainty about the outcomes and direction of their programs, as well as a few outright cries for help.

Chapter Three

Elementary and Middle School Latin Programs

The activity in Latin at the elementary- and middle-school levels forms the most encouraging—and perhaps the most surprising—chapter of this report.

The Inner City Programs

During the 1960's, when educational leaders were searching for ways to improve language skills among economically and culturally deprived students in inner city school districts, the idea of using Latin as a vehicle occurred to some persuasive and influential administrators. Judith LeBovit, in the early 1960's, initiated a strong and effective Foreign Languages in the Elementary School (FLES) Latin program in Washington, D.C., which was later curtailed because of school-system decentralization. Subsequently, Rudolph Masciantonio in Philadelphia, Albert Baca in Los Angeles, and Richard Gascoyne in New York State have established or encouraged large, successful programs that continue to flourish and serve as models for new projects.

Philadelphia

In 1987, Philadelphia had about 12,000 students studying Latin in grades four to six under itinerant and classroom teachers. The program, begun in 1968, has been effective in expanding the English vocabulary and reading skills of urban students of all backgrounds and abilities. In 1979, the district began a program of training classroom teachers in order to supplement and expand the existing program. The training of these paraclassicists, originally funded by grants from the NEH, is now part of the inservice coursework that the district offers for salary credit; in this way, the supply of trained teachers, which now stands at about a hundred, is regularly renewed.

Los Angeles

The Los Angeles Transfer Program, which was begun in 1974 and is no longer dependent on government funding, finances its own teacher training program by offering workshops and materials for other districts. These materials, which are based on the Philadelphia curriculum, are augmented by a Spanish language component and consist of student readers and workbooks, tapes, visual cards, filmstrips, game kits and a teacher's guide. The training of volunteer classroom teachers includes background information about the Latin language, Roman culture, mythology, linguistics, and teaching methods and strategies.

The program has spread beyond the Los Angeles area. In 1982, approximately 3,000 students in grades four through eight were exposed to Latin and the classical heritage through the Language Transfer Program. In 1987, the Los Angeles district system provided training for 75 teachers in 34 Los Angeles schools, as well as for teachers in several school districts in New York State, Missouri and South Carolina.

Expansion

Yet another adaptation of the Philadelphia program is the Latin Cornerstone Project of New York City. Funded by the National Endowment for the Humanities in 1982, this program trains classroom teachers to use materials that include written Latin, etymology, an expanded grammar component, as well as cultural material. Similar programs exist in Baltimore, Chicago, Dade County (Florida), Ft. Worth, Houston, New Castle County (Delaware), New Orleans and Oakland. Cincinnati and Indianapolis use a combination of paraclassicists and certified Latin teachers. According to Rudolph Masciantonio, Director of Foreign Language Education for the Philadelphia School District, hundreds of smaller districts and individual schools have either started or are considering programs in Latin for elementary school children.

Objectives of the Programs

The goals of these various programs include the improvement of English vocabulary, an increased awareness of language structures, the broadening of cultural horizons, an understanding of Roman culture, a heightened interest in learning foreign languages, the improvement of self-concept and, of course, learning some Latin. A considerable body of research confirms the success of such programs in all these areas (articles listed at end of book, p. 75).

Perhaps even more heartening than the compelling research on these programs is the opinions of some students (in response to questionnaires about the New York and California programs):

–"I'm glad I found out how English makes so many words from Latin roots... ."

–"I like saying the Latin words when we do questions and answers."

–"I'm much better at spelling now!"

–"My favorite part was learning what kind of houses, food and clothes they had."

–"Latin is easy for me because I know Spanish."

–"I never was interested in words before, but Latin makes them fun."

NEH Summer Institutes

Besides the substantial support that the NEH has furnished to the elementary programs, the Endowment has also funded, and continues to fund, summer institutes for intensive study of classics by elementary- and middle-school teachers. The fact that professors from the finest graduate departments in the country are happily choosing to spend their summers to work with elementary and middle-school teachers is an encouraging sign of the liveliness of the profession at both of these levels. These institutes provide an opportunity for intellectual enrichment and effect a valuable interaction between the college educators and school teachers. One of the most welcome benefits of these institutes is the camaraderie with colleagues from all over the country that develops from a shared excitement in the serious study of the classics. Teachers report that these NEH summer institutes have completely revitalized their careers.

In 1984, sixty elementary school teachers and librarians participated in the Odyssey Institute. Professor Joseph O'Connor of Georgetown University conceived the idea of introducing a major classical literary work into the elementary curriculum by inviting, under the auspices of the NEH, the sixty participants to two summers of intensive study of the *Odyssey* under his direction. In 1986, the *Aeneid* Institute invited forty elementary-school teachers to explore Vergil's epic poem and design teaching materials to bring its excitement and timeless beauty to their students. (These materials are now available from the Teaching Materials and Resource Center of the ACL.) Another important component of this project was a mentor program, through which the elementary teachers were paired with experienced classicists in their own areas to ensure the continued possibility of fruitful collaboration. Another component of this institute was an introduction to the Latin language and the presentation of the *First Latin* curriculum (published by Longman Press), an outgrowth of the New York Cornerstone project.

In the summer of 1989, another forty elementary school teachers were brought together with university professors and master teachers at Miami University in Oxford, Ohio, to read and study the mythological stories in Ovid's *Metamorphoses*. As these institutes, with the support of the NEH, continue to be offered to teachers at all levels, hundreds of American teachers can enjoy the opportunity of serious study with well known scholars and improve the quality of their own teaching significantly.

Reporting back to their institute directors, teachers said that they—and as a result, their students—loved the challenge, the substance, and the universality of these classic works. They reported that their students were delighted by the adventure and fantasy, and that they identified with the heroes' struggles and wrenching choices between duty and selfishness. As they listened to and read these great works with their teachers, they were invited to consider the nature of heroism and the relative merits of wealth, strength, family, honesty, cunning, and love of country. Teachers felt that the introduction of classics on this level was not only appropriate, but highly motivating and challenging to every kind of student.

The *Aeneid* Institute teachers brought back the fruits of their summer labors to students from kindergarten to grade six; to compensatory and gifted students; to public and private school students; and to students in self-contained classrooms and departmentalized programs. They met at various classical conferences to exchange ideas and give continued mutual support. The group felt strongly that their association should be sustained and perpetuated.

Elementary Teachers of Classics

Out of this resolve arose the organization known as the Elementary Teachers of Classics (ETC), now a standing committee of the American Classical League. The stated purposes of the organization are:

- to nurture and support the teaching of Classics at the elementary level

- to provide a forum for intellectual stimulation, dialogue and development
- to participate in and sponsor conferences and seminars
- to disseminate teaching materials appropriate to elementary curricula

The ETC organization offers Activity Packets for Classics Clubs which are designed to provide a variety of easy-to-use classroom-tested materials related to classics, Latin word study and etymology. To date more than 630 of these Classics Clubs have been established. In the spring of 1990, the ETC sponsored its First Annual National Mythology Exam and had a gratifying response of more than 3400 participants. The ETC also publishes *Prima,* an excellent journal full of ideas and opportunities for elementary teachers, and distributed to all members of the ACL.

Materials

Excellent materials for teaching Latin at the elementary- and middle-school levels are readily available. Some stress English word skills, while others emphasize language awareness or cultural material. Still others concentrate on teaching the Latin language, and several try to combine all these aspects. The School District of Philadelphia and the Los Angeles Unified School District have made their materials available at cost. The *Ecce Romani* series and the *Cambridge Latin Course* are widely used at the 7th and 8th grade levels, while other middle school materials currently in use are *First Latin, Latin is Fun,* and *The Phenomenon of Language.* Also, traditional high-school texts like Jenney's *First Year Latin* and *Latin for Americans* are often used in middle schools that teach Latin, Level I, over a two-year period. The Teaching Materials and Resource Center of the ACL at Miami University in Oxford, Ohio, offers a wealth of inexpensive supplementary material by mail order. Among the small but increasing number of parents who are choosing to educate their children at home during their elementary and middle school years, the programmed *Artes Latinae* series is often chosen as appropriate to this type of education.

Learning Latin

Although many elementary programs do not espouse the learning of the Latin language as their primary goal, it is often the element that students like best. They enjoy pronouncing the sounds of a new language (often learning phonics for the first time); they practice question and answer patterns; they are gently introduced to the concepts of inflection and sentence structure. Besides concepts of person, number and tense, subject and object, they learn numbers, colors, names of family members and a basic vocabulary that enables them to read sentences and enjoy stories in Latin. Some school districts, such as those in New York State, have articulated a fully described program from grades 4-12; in most cases, elementary-school Latin is seen as a springboard—for further Latin study, for modern language study, and/or for all ensuing academic work.

Middle School

Perhaps the most crucial age group of the student clientele for Latin is in the middle schools. There are several current configurations in·the schooling of 11-14 year-olds (e.g. grades 5-8, 6-8 and 7-8), and in almost all states, educational materials and methods for the middle schools are differentiated from those employed in elementary and high schools.

Because the middle-school years are an ideal time for the introduction of new courses and new fields of endeavor, Latin can make a very attractive and useful contribution to the curriculum at this level. Latin is particularly appropriate for the middle schools, since it enhances basic reading and word skills that affect the students' total academic performance and provide an excellent foundation for high school work in general. Administrators and parents, consequently, welcome the introduction of a solid discipline like Latin that by its very nature helps students, at this crucial period in their development, with study skills and the understanding of linguistic concepts.

Many private and some public schools require two or three years of Latin in the middle-school years. This sequence provides the opportunity to accomplish the proven gains in SAT scores that a three year sequence maximizes, brings about improved all-around academic performance, and also establishes an excellent foundation for further study in Latin. Students who complete Latin, Level I, in a two-year time period often assimilate and understand the material better than those who complete it in one high-school year. Latin educators should strive, therefore, to introduce Latin instruction into every middle school and to build their programs upward from there. Middle-school students are enthusiastic, eager to try new things, and often sorely in need of the very benefits that Latin offers. This is the currently critical area where classicists need to enlighten counselors, parents and administrators better than previously, provide qualified teachers and establish attractive programs.

Spreading the Good News

What is necessary now, it seems, is to make the general public aware, through national news coverage, of the advantages of including Latin in the elementary– and middle-school curriculum. It is clear from a number of research studies that this has the effect of improving academic performance among all types of students, including the "students at risk" who are presently such a concern to the nation. But although a movement to extend Latin studies at these levels must involve parents and administrators, the leadership must come from professional classicists. Teachers of Latin at the college and high-school levels should be vocal and persuasive proponents in establishing programs at the elementary and middle-school levels, but they should also be willing supporters and consultants once these programs are established.

Chapter Four

High School Latin Programs

High school Latin enrollments in the United States plummeted from 702,000 in 1962 to 150,000 in 1976. Since 1977 there has been a slow and steady increase, and at the present time all the signs point to continued vigor and growth. It would be a great mistake for us at this point to forget our brush with extinction—or to ignore the creative and heroic efforts that have provided Latin with a new lease on life. Latin will continue to be taught only as long as American students choose to study it.

According to figures from the American Council on the Teaching of Foreign Languages (ACTFL) for 1985 (latest national statistics available), 176,841 students were enrolled in American public high-school Latin classes; some estimate an equal number in private schools. Other indications of numerical growth are enrollments in the ACL/NJCL National Latin Exam (from 9,000 in 1978 to 71,000 in 1990), participation in the National Junior Classical League (NJCL) (51,500 in 1990), yearly increases in ACL membership (3800 in 1990) and attendance at ACL Institutes and Workshops, and a slow but steady increase in the number of students taking the Advanced Placement Latin Examinations (2712 in 1990).

Student Preparation

Today's Latin student population is indeed a "mixed bag"—national merit finalists and learning disabled students; aspiring artists and athletes; those who have, or have not, succeeded at learning a modern foreign language; those whose first language is not English; the busy, the bored, and the conscientious; and among all these, a number who are mightily excited about learning Latin. The mixture makes teaching Latin very exciting—and very challenging.

Teachers report that many of their high school students bring little or no knowledge of English grammar to their study of Latin, that they do not read books, and that they spend significantly less time on homework than students of previous decades. Shorter attention span, passivity and superficiality are mentioned as the result of thousands of hours of television watching. Jobs, cars and time-consuming extra-curricular activities compete for students' attention. At the same time, they share their generation's expectation for a quick and practical pay-off for their efforts. Students at all levels seem to be getting less attention and guidance from their parents, and the schools apparently are not structured to compensate for this deficiency. Some teachers perceive students as possessing obvious, basic educational and emotional needs that prevent them from learning Latin or their other subjects. Many teachers state that it requires great energy and unrelenting effort to get and keep students' attention, to motivate them to work and to keep them on course. Perhaps this is nothing new. All conscientious teachers have always taken on this daily labor of Sisyphus!

It would be incorrect, however, to leave the impression that all students fit the profile of the contemporary student drawn above. Teachers find motivated and talented students in every classroom. The high quality of the top scorers on the Advanced Placement Examinations, the winners in the competitions at the National Junior Classical League Conventions, and the medal winners of the ACL/NJCL National Latin Exam are ample proof of the high caliber of teaching going on in many secondary schools. That classes are often a mix of the motivated and unmotivated does, however, make the task harder for the Latin teacher of the 1990's.

Despite the challenges offered by today's students, Latin teachers state that they are willing and even happy to "take students from where they are." Many teachers are sustained by a very high level of enjoyment, and even love, of their subject. Of all the reasons for studying and teaching Latin, perhaps the most compelling (which is admittedly difficult to communicate to the uninitiated) is the richness and challenge of the language and literature itself.

Besides the aforementioned considerations of students and the subject matter, teachers have also commented on the following aspects of their day-to-day efforts.

Trying to Do It All

The most frustrating aspect of teaching Latin today, according to our respondents, concerns the substance and pace of the curriculum. Veteran teachers say that they cover less material in their textbooks than they used to, and that they worry seriously about their students' mastery of the material. On the one hand, they are dealing with students who are less willing to do homework, which means almost all learning, practice and review must be done in class; on the other hand, teachers feel compelled by prevailing trends to enrich their classes by teaching more mythology, Roman culture and history, to say nothing of basic English sentence structure. Since an overwhelming number of students have stated that they are taking Latin for the express purpose of improving their SAT verbal scores, teachers also feel pressured to do more work with etymology.

Isolation and Overload

One of the most common difficulties mentioned by Latin teachers is the sense of isolation many feel. Rarely do Latin teachers have a colleague in their school; sometimes, they do not even have one in their city or county. However, one positive consequence of being the only teacher of Latin in a school is the opportunity to form close bonds with one's students, who then often continue their Latin study for three or four years. A very large number of our respondents (70%) reported that they had other teaching and/or administrative responsibilities besides Latin, and many reported that they travel between two or more schools each day. A large number expressed a yearning for the sense of professional community that exists in other departments in their schools; they regretted the lack of opportunity to take refresher courses, to attend workshops on new methods and materials, or simply to talk with other teachers of Latin.

The Numbers Game

Only in rare and enviable instances do schools require Latin. In almost all public schools, Latin is offered as an elective, and teachers' jobs depend on the number of students who sign up for their classes. Latin teachers often find themselves in the role of recruiters, scrambling for that one more body to make the minimum number for a Latin, Level I or II, class. This is not new; since the 1930's, Latin teachers have had to exert special efforts to keep their subject in the curriculum. The current (and welcome) emphasis on modern foreign languages makes yet another claim on students' limited time. This "numbers crunch" also forces teachers to consider keeping even poor students, with the result that some third and fourth year students, though loyal, know very little Latin. This situation threatens the standards of the advanced class and encourages "watering down" to accommodate those who simply cannot or will not keep up with the work.

Miscellaneous Problems From All Quarters

This last list represents a "grab bag" of difficulties that were reported by numerous teachers from across the nation.

- difficulty among non-native speakers of English in understanding teachers (most Latin teachers rely on giving explanations in English)
- poor English skills among many native speakers
- antiquated and sluggish textbook adoption procedures
- the necessity of teaching several levels in one class period
- wide range of ability levels in one class: gifted as well as remedial
- the grouping of Advanced Placement students with regular track students
- upper level students unable to fit Latin into their schedule
- significant loss of teaching time due to classroom interruptions
- teaching students with scheduling problems before and after school and during lunch periods
- requiring even beginning teachers to teach all levels of Latin (including Advanced Placement) whether prepared or not

What Latin teachers must do in this age of "classics for everyone" is to attempt to raise the level of achievement of the greatest number to the highest possible point, and provide something of value for each student. When this requires compromises, as it very often does, teachers often agonize over the decisions that must be made.

Types of Latin Programs

Many classifications are possible: rural vs. urban, private vs. public, large vs. small, two-year vs. four-year sequence, required vs. elective program, Advanced Placement vs. non-Advanced Placement, etc. Generally speaking, the survey showed surprisingly little difference among these programs from the point of view of curricular expectations. Frequently, the success of a given Latin program depends more on the expectations and commitment of the individual Latin teacher than on the type of school or student body.

Private School vs. Public

Although important differences were apparent between these two categories, our survey actually showed more similarity than difference between their Latin programs. Private school students, like their public school mates, valued the study of Latin primarily for its relevance to the acquisition of English language skills. Many of them also espoused the traditional view of Latin study as a valuable tool to promote clear and precise thinking. More private school than public school students, however, identified the reading of Latin literature in the original Latin as an important goal. About sixty percent of the private schools responding to our survey required Latin of their students, often at the middle-school level. Teachers in private schools felt that they experienced greater autonomy and less administrative and bureaucratic interference than their public school colleagues, yet many remarked that they recognized and regretted their isolation from Latin-teaching colleagues in other private or public schools.

Materials

New materials of various kinds and at all levels have appeared on the Latin scene and continue to do so with regularity. Many programs continue to use traditional grammar/ translation textbooks (and their revisions) such as Jenney's *Latin I - IV, Latin for Americans, Our Latin Heritage,* and *Living Latin.* There is also a significant trend toward the use of reading programs like the *Cambridge Latin Course* and Longman's *Ecce Romani* series. In the reading programs, the goal of reading comprehension is placed before that of learning grammatical forms and rules. Materials used in reading programs are easily accessible to a wide range of students and offer readings and exercises that hold greater intrinsic interest than many of the unconnected, single-sentence exercises in traditional textbooks. The reading textbooks teach the language through a series of interconnected stories, with questions and translation exercises based on the stories. Grammatical principles are explained and learned inductively. Traditional books often emphasize the learning of vocabulary from lists and the learning of forms and grammar from explanations and practice exercises, with reading as a delayed goal. While both approaches are designed to lead students to the reading of Latin literature, proponents of traditional methods argue that their students have a better grammatical foundation, and reading-text enthusiasts claim that their students read Latin sooner and with greater ease and appreciation.

Methodology

National trends in pedagogy and educational reform are based on research that shows students learn better when they are actively and emotionally involved, participating in group work, games, performance activities and imaginative projects. Latin teachers who employ these methods report that this type of teaching does create excitement in their classes and also builds larger enrollments. The reverse side of this coin, however, is that such techniques and activities do not fit very well with the teaching of basic morphology and syntax, which many teachers still view as the *sine qua non* of the Latin classroom. Teachers say that it takes time to teach children how to learn in groups, to pursue research topics and to create art projects; they also sometimes feel that this time is stolen from their grammar lessons. Although creative projects often stand out in students' minds as the most exciting aspect of their Latin study, many teachers report that these activities exacerbate the pressure they feel to finish the prescribed linguistic content of the course.

General Description of Levels

Although programs differ from place to place and from school to school, the outline below reflects the general trends in Latin as it is taught in today's high schools.

• *Latin I & II* The first two years of Latin cover all the major grammatical points of the language, as well as the forms of nouns, adjectives, pronouns and verbs. In the first year, students read "made Latin" sentences and stories, as well as passages and proverbs in real Latin. The prescribed list of what is to be covered in the first year as opposed to the second year is determined in most programs by the order of presentation in the textbook used. Roman culture and mythology are very popular with students and are included in virtually all programs. Some Roman history and geography are taught, and most teachers said that they spend some part of every class on English word study. Many teachers said that they tried to read some connected Latin prose or "easy" Latin poetry during the second year. Which authors are read is determined by what is included in the textbook available; Caesar is still preferred by many, but most reported reading a smaller quantity of this author than they had previously. The appearance of many short readers with facing vocabularies, full notes and truly useful teachers' manuals has given teachers and students a much wider selection of readings to choose from, both on the lower and upper levels.

• *Latin III* A great deal of diversity exists at this level. Alternative approaches include:

- a traditional year of Latin prose with emphasis on Cicero' s Catilinarians in addition to presentation of advanced grammar (Some teachers said the Catilinarians were both too difficult and too sophisticated for their students.)

- continued use of second-year textbook until grammar lessons are completed

- introduction of other authors such as Plautus, Ovid, Petronius, Tacitus, or from Medieval Latin, often through short readers containing complete or excerpted, original or slightly adapted works annotated for high school use

- Advanced Placement (AP) Syllabus for Vergil or Catullus/Horace (If students in a four-year program want the opportunity to take both AP Exams, they must do one in the third year. 45% of those teachers who have AP programs are experimenting with this third year option, and many teachers have expressed concern that "regular" students cannot perform at this level and should not be forced into AP courses.)

- anthology of prose and poetry readings combined with grammar review

The majority of teachers did agree that in the third year only authentic Latin texts should be read, and that the reviewing of morphology and syntax should be systematically continued in tandem with the reading.

• *Latin IV* The reading of Latin texts continues, often consisting of the major part of books I, II, IV, and VI of Vergil's *Aeneid.* Many teachers stated that they were not able to complete even three books, but they felt that reading two books was possible and appropriate for fourth-year students. Some complained that the rush to complete the AP Syllabus deprived their classes of the time for discussion that they felt was more beneficial and meaningful to their students than merely "finishing the lines." Other teachers stated that they preferred to do a survey of Latin authors from all periods, tailoring material especially to the interests of their particular students. There was universal agreement that reteaching and review of basic Latin structures be continued at this level.

Opportunities Available for a Comprehensive Latin Program

Because there are so many excellent activities available for Latin students, it takes only one informed, persuasive and energetic teacher to create a program that is outstanding in his or her school. Students who are fortunate enough to have such teachers can essentially "major in Latin" in some high schools. These programs, which exist in both public and private schools, produce a handful of excellent students, some of whom will be the classical scholars and teachers of the next generation. Success breeds success: administrative, parental and community support can be developed to help when there is a need for publicity, fund-raising, chaperoning and transportation. The top students of the school are easily drawn into these "super" programs because of the opportunities for challenge, competition, recognition and excellence. Even small schools, including schools that offer only two years of Latin, can offer many of these opportunities to Latin students. Among the offerings of an "ideal" Latin program are:

- School Latin Club and/or Latin Honor Society
- Advanced Placement course(s)
- participation in the Junior Classical League
- ACL/NJCL National Latin Exam
- NJCL Honor Society
- CEEB Latin Achievement Test
- regional, state and local contests
- NJCL Essay Contest
- interschool competitions such as Latin Bowl (Certamen)
- field trips to museums and galleries
- daily tutoring available from teacher or peers
- news of Latin activities in school and local publications

(and in very special programs:)

- four or five year sequence
- one or more years of Greek study
- summer Latin academy/camp program
- optional travel to Europe

Standardized Testing on the High School Level

Renewed interest in Latin study and the recent wider variety of teaching methods have given a new impetus to a variety of standardized tests available to Latin students.

• *AP Examinations.* Each year more high schools choose to participate in the College Board's Advanced Placement program. In 1990, the Vergil and Lyric Examinations were taken by 1887 and 825 students respectively. Most colleges and universities offer course credit in

Latin for a passing grade in these examinations. It is worthy of note that the number of lines in the Vergil syllabus has been cut twice in recent years (from 2649 lines in 1980 to 1842 lines in 1990) and now includes excerpts from books I, II and VI, and Book IV in its entirety. These cuts were made after it was discovered that the AP Syllabus was requiring more of high school students than the majority of college syllabi for the same author(s). By cutting the total number of lines, the AP Development Committee also hoped to allow more class time for discussion of the lines as literature.

The first part of the exam (45%), consisting of questions on several sight passages, has always proved very difficult for students; the second part (55%) is composed of essay questions based on passages from the prescribed syllabus. The Advanced Placement program offers the exceptional student an excellent academic opportunity and has great appeal for ambitious high school students and their teachers. There were, however, several problem areas that teachers reported:

- Since the examination is administered early in May, it is very difficult to finish the syllabus (especially for the *Aeneid*); there is not sufficient time for analysis, discussion and review.
- Some teachers object that Horace is too difficult and sophisticated for high school students. (Alternatives are presently being considered.)
- Most schools can offer only one course on the advanced level, and not all students are capable of AP work; poorer students are often "dragged along" unwilling or unable to do the work.

• *The ACL/NJCL National Latin Exam.*   In addition to the *Classical Outlook* and the annual ACL Institute and Workshops for Latin teachers, the American Classical League sponsors the National Latin Exam (NLE), which was created to answer the need for a norm-referenced test for all American students. Dr. Paul Warsley's *Auxilium Latinum* had filled this role until the 1960's, after which he was unable to continue the examination. The NLE, first administered in 1977 to 9,000 participants, was taken by 71,500 in 1990. Six levels are offered, from *Introduction to Latin* through *Latin,* Level V. These examinations offer Latin students an opportunity to join thousands of other Latin students in a nationwide event, to win awards, and to gain recognition for Latin in their schools and in their communities. An extensive scholarship program helps gold medal winners pursue their Latin studies in college.

As a result of consultation with teachers, the NLE Syllabus was modified in 1988 to reflect the fact that the examination is administered in March rather than at the end of the year. A number of items that had been tested on the Latin I and II levels were moved to the Latin II and III levels, respectively. Many teachers report that this examination has created a sense of national involvement in a common goal, improved motivation among their students and filled the need for a national measure of all their best students' achievements.

• *Other Tests and Contests.*   The College Board Achievement Test score is offered by students for consideration for admission to the colleges of their choice. It, too, has undergone considerable change since 1980. At that time, a survey of American high school teachers showed that the existing test did not reflect either the objectives or realities of students' achievement. The current revised version of the Latin Achievement Test is geared to students who have completed from two to four years of study and contains items that represent a broad range of linguistic structures and readings typical of all four years of Latin study.

Besides the Latin Achievement Test, the AP Examinations, and the National Latin Exam, other competitions of many sorts add liveliness and challenge to Latin study on the secondary level:

- national and regional essay contests
- scholarship translation contests
- state and local grammar contests
- "Certamen" and Latin Bowl competitions
- local and state oratorical contests
- art, costume and sports contests
- numerous competitions of these and other kinds at state and national JCL conventions

Difficulty of Constructing Standardized Tests at Lower Levels

As a result of the widely differing teaching materials and strategies in use today, creating a common evaluating process for the lower levels is very difficult. Teachers using *Ecce Romani* and the *Cambridge Latin Course* complained that the National Latin Exam and/or their state tests do not offer their students sufficient opportunity to use the reading skills that are stressed in their approach. Teachers of traditional textbooks complained that there is not enough emphasis on grammar and analysis.

Developing examinations based on reading passages presents problems because of the differing vocabularies and orders of grammatical presentation used in the different programs. As examples of the wide divergence among beginning programs, we may note that one program uses only first- and second-conjugation verbs during the first year; another introduces all four conjugations and the irregular verbs in the earliest lessons; some present the passive voice and present participles in the first year, others in the second. Likewise, teaching the uses of the subjunctive is done by some in the first year, by some in the second, and by others in the third year.

Current practice in standardized testing seems to be trying to accommodate these differences by compromise and inclusion of a variety of types of test items. It becomes somewhat easier after Latin I and II. There seems to be general agreement that whatever textbooks are used, Latin students should have been introduced to the major grammatical constructions and enough forms and vocabulary to read Latin texts in Latin III.

Computers and the Electronic Classroom

Although some interesting and useful software has been developed for use by Latin students, the computer has not yet had a noticeable impact on high-school Latin. Most of the programs provide practice drill for noun or verb forms, consolidation of vocabulary, etc. As each new generation of students becomes more accustomed to using the computer for school work, Latin students and teachers will be looking for and perhaps producing new instructional and enrichment software.

Distance learning is becoming more common in many high schools, especially those in areas with small populations or limited resources. Latin, being a minority subject, seems a natural choice for this technology, especially in schools where only a few students want Latin or where no qualified Latin teacher can be found. Although there is no substitute for the direct interaction between teacher and student, the electronic classroom can provide an opportunity for Latin study where no other exists. In the state of Virginia, for example, there are two separate long-distance video programs (interactive with telephone talkback and fax machine) that provide daily instruction to more than three hundred students in forty-two high schools. This technology needs to be considered on a case-to-case basis from several points of view, but can be advantageous in certain situations.

Latin and the Modern Languages

Since Latin teachers sometimes also teach modern languages, and since Latin teachers in most schools are part of the foreign language department, it is no surprise that many Latin teachers establish close ties with their modern language colleagues. Latin teachers report that this interaction can be quite beneficial. Research and pedagogical developments in the modern language field can bring welcome variety to Latin classrooms. Foreign Language Week, holidays and similar celebrations encourage inter-language projects that build an esprit de corps among teachers and students. It is impossible to overstate the importance of the role of requirements (state, local, college admission) to foreign language study in this country. Inasmuch as Latin falls under the rubric of "foreign language," it is in the best interest of Latin teachers to nurture and strengthen the bonds with their foreign language colleagues and with their national, regional and local foreign language associations.

Help and Support for Latin Teachers

Latin teachers at every level in this country are among the most fortunate in the world because of the excellent support organizations and opportunities available to them. First among Latin teachers' organizations is the American Classical League (ACL), which comprises 3,800 high-school and college teachers. The ACL publishes the *Classical Outlook*, a journal for teachers of Classics at all levels, which contains articles, reports, materials, reviews, and other timely information. This is an excellent, high-quality publication that no Latin teacher should be without. In late June, the ACL holds an annual institute for teachers, with a program of workshops and papers, where teachers from all over the United States and Canada can come together and share ideas and friendship.

The American Philological Association

Latin teachers at every level also benefit from membership in the American Philological Association (APA), which since it was founded in 1869, is one of the oldest professional organizations in the United States. The APA publishes annual *Transactions* with superb research articles by leading classicists, and the APA's Division of Education periodically publishes Education Papers that frequently preserve the proceedings of the special panels on classical education planned by the Division of Education and presented at the APA's Annual Meetings. With support from the NEH, the APA joined with the ACL to form the Joint Committee on the Classics in American Education (JCCAE), a committee that grew out of the very successful 1986 conference of teachers, administrators, and laypeople on the Classics in American Schools. The report of this conference, *The Classics in American Schools: Teaching the Ancient World*, contains a wealth of information concerning the teaching of classical subjects across the curriculum and is highly recommended as additional reading to the readers of this report. It has been widely distributed by the APA and is invaluable to teachers, parents and administrators in their efforts to support or initiate programs in Latin, Greek, and/or Classical Civilization.

NEH Support for the Classics

The National Endowment for the Humanities (NEH) offers financial support on a national level for the teaching of Latin at all levels. These programs have included institutes for the training of Latin teachers, sabbatical programs for teachers, and study programs for high school students. The NEH also sponsors up to sixty 4-6 week seminars each summer on a variety of texts and topics in the humanities. Each seminar provides fifteen teachers with the opportunity to work under the direction of a distinguished teacher and active scholar in the field of the seminar. During the summer of 1990, topics included were "Homer's *Iliad* and *Odyssey*," "Cicero: Moral and Political Aspirations," and "The Classical Heritage of Medieval European Literature." High-school teachers report that the experience of studying with these outstanding university scholars in the summer seminars is exhilarating, inspiring and revitalizing. The extraordinary importance of these NEH programs to the on-going success of the classics in America cannot be overestimated, and classicists have every reason both to lobby for legislative appropriations and taxpayer support of the NEH as well as to take advantage of the opportunities that NEH funding provides them.

State and Local Associations

In most cases, the easiest place for teachers to find support and fellowship is in their local, state or regional classical associations. Where none exists, a few enthusiastic teachers may form one. In these associations, even if they are small (perhaps because they are small), elementary-, middle-, and high-school teachers can meet and share ideas with their own colleagues, as well as with the classics faculty of their nearest college or university.

Other Helpful Organizations and Publications

The Classical Association of the Middle West and South (CAMWS) is the largest of the regional classical associations and currently includes teachers of classics from 34 American states and Canadian provinces among its members. Besides publishing the *Classical Journal,* the CAMWS holds annual meetings and provides grants, prizes and recognition of several kinds for its member teachers and their students. The CAMWS also has a Committee for the Promotion of Latin (CPL) that provides publicity aids, ideas for improving public relations and promotional funds to Latin teachers.

The ACL National Committee for Latin and Greek (NCLG), with financial support from the ACL and other leading North American and international classical organizations, works with the Joint National Committee for Languages to lobby at the federal level for the classical languages and to advertise Latin, Greek and Classical Humanities among administrators and laypeople with occasional flyers, its bi-annual *Prospects* newsletter and articles regularly placed in the popular press.

Besides the ACL's *Classical Outlook* and *Prima,* the APA's *Transactions* and Education Papers, the publication of the Classical Association of the Atlantic States (CAAS) called *Classical World* (particularly useful for its annual surveys of textbooks and audio-visual aids) and that of the Vergilian Society called *Vergilius,* there are numerous other periodicals and newsletters available to teachers that make the teaching of Latin, Greek and/or ancient civilization livelier and easier. A few of these are the *New England Classical Newsletter & Journal* (particularly useful for its frequent notes and articles on Latin pedagogy), *theJ.A.C.T. Review* (particularly useful for its up-to-date reviews of textbooks published in Great Britain). Available for students are the very popular *Pompeiiana Newsletter,* the British *Omnibus,* the bi-monthly magazine *Calliope* (on ancient history), *Classics Chronicle* (a publication which draws connections between modern Europe and the Roman empire), and the colorful comicbook-format magazines, *Adulescens* and *Iuvenis.*

To conclude our discussion of the high school level, our survey proves that Latin continues to be appropriate, practical and beneficial for students at this stage of their development. As a result of several factors—the substantial and challenging subject matter, the considerable potential for linguistic and cultural transfer, the small-group fellowship, the dedication of committed, hard-working Latin teachers—the Latin class becomes for some students the most memorable of all in their high school experience.

Chapter Five

Latin on the
College/University Level

Areas of Growth

The information and conclusions in this chapter are based on the NLG sub-committee's 1988 survey of 210 post-secondary institutions, a 1989 follow-up survey, and a number of panel-audience discussions at meetings of the ACL, APA and CAMWS. Our inquiries revealed that today's classics departments have not slipped into a collection of irrelevant, obscure specialists, but are prospering and visible on college and university campuses across the country.

A number of important changes have occurred in recent decades. A growing number of students who have had no previous exposure to classics are choosing to study classical languages and civilization for the first time in college or university. On the classical civilization side of the curriculum, this has meant a number of popular new courses taught in English, such as Greek and Roman mythology, Greek and Roman civilization, classical archaeology, literature in translation, Greek and Latin etymology, medical terminology, and topics courses like *Women in Antiquity, Ancient Technology* and *Ancient Sports.* Most students elect these courses to fulfill a humanities distribution requirement and may take only one such course in the classics department, but others become especially interested in the subject and go on to learn more about the ancient world. Another healthy sign in many post-secondary institutions is the increase in collaborative efforts with elementary, middle and secondary schools.

A growing number of colleges are now offering a Classics major with a concentration in Classical Humanities (also called Classical Civilization or Classical Studies) that includes a selection of courses in English on the ancient world as well as a Latin or Greek language component (usually a two-year sequence). This concentration appeals to students with interest in a liberal arts degree, and often to those who plan to continue their education in professional schools. When asked about Classical Humanities as a concentration within the Classics major, students gave the following reasons for their choice:

- high interest in the subject matter
- improvement of English skills
- higher GRE scores
- presentation of a more substantial transcript to graduate school

Today's College Student

The risk of oversimplification is always present when describing an age group across the nation, but a number of studies, as well as the results of our own survey, have given us an interesting general profile. Today's college students are not so well prepared, or so willing, or so able to learn as their predecessors. They are described as a "TV generation" that has done little serious reading, with resulting poor vocabulary and inadequate facility with the extended, connected prose that is required for completion and full comprehension of college reading assignments.

A survey published by the Higher Education Research Institute of UCLA states that more than 25% of freshmen entering in 1989 needed remedial help in math; of students surveyed from freshmen to seniors, only 10% did extra reading for any course; only 54% had visited a museum or art gallery in the past year; almost half reported earning a varsity letter in sports; many reported holding jobs that claimed ten hours or more a week of their time, energy and attention. Almost a quarter planned to major in business, while about 8% were interested in schoolteaching as a career. It is significant that, while their readiness for college work was questionable, their high school grades were better than ever. "Grade inflation" seems to be at its zenith, still another indication of the need for improvement of quality in American education.

Reasons for Choosing Latin

Our survey indicated that college students elected Latin for their language requirement chiefly for the following reasons, with no significant order of priority:

- they wanted to read Latin literature in the original Latin
- they hoped to improve their reading and writing skills in English
- they were interested in the life and culture of the Romans

In effect, college students choosing to study Latin have a practical regard for its ability to improve their test scores and enrich their transcripts, while at the same time they have a genuine interest in classical civilization and its literature.

College Latin Programs

Latin and Greek majors today often begin their study of Latin and almost always of Greek in college or at the university. In the past, most majors would have arrived with three or four years of high-school Latin behind them and would have begun their college level work with beginning Greek and advanced Latin literature courses. The student of today who begins Latin in college will probably not graduate with the level of linguistic competence that an earlier start would have produced.

The majority of students enrolled in Latin classes on the college level have done so, as they did in classical civilization courses, to fulfill institutional requirements. Our survey revealed that there are two basic types of beginning programs:

- the traditional grammar/translation course in which the students are marched at a fast clip through Latin grammar in two (or one and a half) semesters using a traditional textbook such as Wheelock's *Latin: An Introductory Course*. Practice exercises from Latin to English and English to Latin are assigned as well as illustrative sentences from Roman authors.

- the reading approach, usually the *Cambridge Latin Course* or the *Ecce Romani* series (but also in use: Oerberg's *Lingua Latina,* the *Oxford Latin Course* and Jones and Sidwell's *Reading Latin*). Some of these texts were originally developed for younger students, but are being used successfully in a number of college level programs. Generally speaking, the reading-approach method is less threatening to the average student and often contributes to increased enrollments.

Teaching Assistants

Since Classics departments are small as a rule, the student planning to major in Latin will most often be in the same classes as the student meeting a two- or four-semester foreign language requirement. In larger institutions elementary Latin courses are taught by graduate teaching assistants. A few respondents voiced concern that some of these graduate students are (understandably) inexperienced, and are sometimes either unable or unmotivated to provide a good beginning for freshmen. Others noted that many large universities could not survive without these teaching assistants, many of whom are excellent teachers by instinct or have had experience teaching in schools. In either case, both graduate teaching assistants and their students will benefit greatly from the supervision, suggestions and encouragement of veteran department members. This pedagogical training can and should be very useful to these assistants in their subsequent professional lives.

Slower Pace

Latin students are not exempt from the typical student profile of poor preparation, with less time and enthusiasm for study. Our respondents specifically mentioned deficiencies in college students' knowledge of English grammar, ability to memorize, and powers of analysis—skills especially useful for learning Latin. As a result, more than half the survey respondents said that their college classes were proceeding at a slower rate than their beginning classes of former years.

Other changes our survey noted in the teaching of Latin on the college or university level were:

- more emphasis on cultural material
- greater efforts to impart grammatical principles through reading
- some increase in the use of oral practice
- some increase in the use of computer-assisted instruction

Etymology

English and Latin word study are not particularly stressed in Latin classes on the college level, presumably since many classics departments offer separate etymology courses, either in Greek and Latin word roots generally or in scientific terminology. Notwithstanding the availability of these other courses, and their usefulness to future teachers of Latin, it would seem that Latin courses that give express attention to the formation of English derivatives come closer to meeting students' expressed reasons for studying Latin.

Materials

Many elements of the reading textbooks such as the *Oxford Latin Course* and the Cambridge University Press's *Reading Latin* cater to the changes in student preference and expectation, a fact that may acccount for their growing popularity. These changes may be suggestive of trends; in general, however, the majority (100 vs. 58 in our survey) of collegiate/ university level Latin classes are based on a traditional grammar/translation textbook like Wheelock's *Latin: An Introductory Course* and Johnston's *Traditio*. The following were suggestions from respondents for improvements and changes they would like to see in Latin textbooks:

- earlier presentation of the subjunctive
- earlier presentation of indirect statement
- introduction of connected prose as soon as possible
- literary selections from a wider range of historical periods
- extensive glossing of vocabulary to enhance reading facility
- simpler and more helpful notes

Entrance and Placement Tests

Concerning the use of placement and proficiency tests by college Classics departments and the awarding of credit for Advanced Placement examinations, our survey showed:

- Most institutions prefer to use their own placement test.
- Fewer use the Latin Achievement Test score for placement than in the past.
- A large number use no test for placement. Usually, in such cases, students are placed after discussion with departmental advisers.

Students who scored well on proficiency examinations were allowed in some cases to fufill their language requirement without coursework; more often, their requirement was reduced from four to two semesters.

Placement

The majority of students entering with two or three years of high-school Latin were placed in intermediate classes; some went into literature courses and some returned to beginning classes. Many of these students had a gap of a year or even two since their high school Latin study, which tended in most cases to diminish the quality of what they had learned. Some of our respondents reported that they had solved the problem of overqualified students enrolling in beginning classes by offering these on a pass/fail basis, thereby discouraging students seeking an "easy A."

AP Credit

Most institutions surveyed (86%) grant college credit for Advance Placement courses taken in high school. The number of students requesting credit for the Advanced Placement examinations in both Vergil and Catullus/Horace has been steadily increasing. There have been three significant reductions in the Advanced Placement Vergil syllabus in the last decade (the most recent in 1990, from 2649 lines to 1842 lines). The quantity of reading prescribed by the high-school AP syllabus is based on Educational Testing Service (ETS) surveys of the amount of reading done in corresponding college courses. This suggests that students at the collegiate level are also completing less than in former years.

Graduate Training: Is It Preparing Candidates for the Positions Available?

The burgeoning of culture courses and the introduction of interdisciplinary courses into the collegiate general (or core or humanities distribution) requirement has resulted in a number of entry-level teaching positions that require candidates to be well trained in fields other than pure classical philology. There is currently a call for college-level teacher candidates who can include, in their teaching and research, current intellectual thought from other disciplines such as literary criticism, semiotics, theater performance, archaeology, anthropology, and psychology. Besides considering some work in these additional areas, graduate students should also be trained in how to teach Latin, since it is quite likely that they may be doing so. This training, which may be part of their preparation for work as teaching assistants, should include the study of current theories of language acquisition and the evolution of methods, strategies and materials for Latin teaching. It is worthy of note that in the last decade, in graduate-level departments of classics, considerably more dissertations have been written by Hellenists than by Latinists, whereas the majority of teaching positions listed by the APA and ACL placement services are designed for candidates with expertise in teaching Latin.

Interaction Between College Classics Departments and Other Levels

Reports of increased and fruitful collaboration between the collegiate and high school levels provide encouraging news for the profession. Most of this interaction takes place at local and state levels. A number of our respondents reported that they belonged to their state classical associations, but many more, especially those whom we did not reach, do not . A sizable number of college-level programs have implemented ways to work with secondary teachers. Efforts in this area include:

- faculty visiting schools to encourage students to continue their Latin studies
- offering courses for Latin teachers (especially on weekends and in the evenings)
- sponsoring teacher workshops
- sponsoring Latin Day activities
- participating in NEH summer seminars for elementary-, middle- and high-school teachers
- becoming participating members of local classical organizations
- teaching pedagogy courses and supervising student teachers

NEH Institutes

An increasing number of outstanding professors of classics are taking advantage of the opportunities offered by the National Endowment for the Humanities to participate in collaborative institutes for teachers of classical subjects at all levels. Besides funding, the NEH provides generous help in formulating ideas for proposals and in their preparation. The teachers who apply to attend these institutes are eager for knowledge, ready to study and work, and dedicated to improving their own teaching with the classical material they gather from these institutes. College professors provide background information for the texts considered, and guidance in the reading and discussion of these texts. For many of the participants, this experience is the beginning of a lifelong interest in particular classical topics. As teachers take their newfound classical knowledge back to their school and students, they create a new enthusiasm for these subjects and help ensure a source of future classicists for years to come. According to professors who have conducted these institutes, the initial obstacles (e.g. intensive reading assignments) are easily outweighed by the intense satisfaction and stimulation teachers discover in their participation.

Parameters of College/University and School Interaction

While their profession needs and expects more collaboration from college-level classicists, difficulties of time and priority do arise. Such services to the profession as those listed above may be viewed with disfavor, or at least neutrally, by institutional peers and administrators. Whether teaching at "research" institutions or traditional liberal arts institutions, classicists are being expected—as are professors in all disciplines—to meet more stringent criteria of research, teaching and service when they seek tenure, promotion or merit increases. Tenure and promotion committees often tend to look more favorably upon papers read at professional meetings than at workshops for teachers. The writing of a new textbook may not be seen to be as valuable as a "more learned" commentary or monograph.

Even though such attitudes may be changing within the classics profession itself, decisions concerning tenure, promotion and awards are largely outside of a department's control (though not necessarily outside of its influence). Under these circumstances, the classics profession might well consider increasing its acknowledgment of service to its own. These active efforts at collaboration among the different levels can only strengthen and enrich the entire profession.

Teaching Responsibilities

Since there is such a wide range of sizes and types of programs, professional classicists have widely differing teaching responsibilities. A faculty member of a small department may teach eight different courses a year, and still be asked to accept an upper level Greek or Latin course as an "overload," in order to maintain the Classics major. In larger departments, faculty may teach fewer courses, but with multiple sections, or with a single large lecture section (100 or more), which presents problems in the quality of personal interaction with students. Teaching assistants give some relief, but at the cost of faculty time in supervising and coordinating their efforts to maintain a high standard of teaching excellence. In small departments with large enrollments, faculty are faced with a combination of the above problems.

Professional Isolation

Members of small Classics departments may have little opportunity to confer with specialists in their area of interest. They may be the only person on campus specializing in antiquity; this is particularly problematic when substantial distances separate them from their colleagues at other institutions. Funding for travel to professional meetings and research is especially important for these remotely situated classicists, but is not always readily available. The APA Committee on Education has recently begun to address this problem of professional isolation by arranging informal meetings of such classicists. A directory of such programs has been compiled as an initial step toward developing channels of communication and the sharing of resources and ideas.

The Problem of Student/Faculty Ratio

Perhaps the most difficult problem now confronting college or university classics departments is the student/faculty ratio. Some departments find their enrollments growing, but are not able to persuade the administration to add teaching positions to their department. In some cases, the faculty may have a semester load of a hundred or more students. Graduate teaching assistants can give some relief, but only if there is a graduate program and if funding is available. Some departments continue to have low or falling enrollments, due to changes in requirements or other factors, while others may have growing enrollments in classical humanities courses and falling enrollments in language courses. It is often a difficult balancing act to meet the teaching needs of students majoring in classics as well as those enrolled in the general education courses in classical civilization. In some situations, departments with small enrollments must fight for administrative support for their programs against the prospect of being merged or subsumed under another department with subsequent loss of autonomy and funding.

Pressures and Obligations of a University Classicist

"Publish or perish" is still the rule in classics departments, especially for untenured members. Ironically, it is during the first five or six years of their teaching that a major publication is demanded if they are to receive tenure; it is during these same years that they will be expected to teach more of the exhausting lower-division courses with large enrollments than their tenured colleagues who have already published extensively. The pressure to publish persists for all faculty and cannot be safely ignored. In any research-oriented department, there is only one thing which counts in salary and promotion reviews—in a word, research.

All Classics faculty are expected to be actively involved in the planning and administration of their departments; this includes committees on undergraduate studies, graduate studies, curriculum and personnel. They are also expected to be involved in university-wide faculty senates and committees on such matters as academic rules, library acquisitions, computer services, general curriculum and instructional technology. An additional responsibility that is both time-consuming and crucial is the advising of undergraduate and graduate students on such matters as courses, careers and jobs. Classics faculty are expected to attend the annual meetings of the APA and/or Archaeological Institute of America (AIA), and often must present research-intensive papers there or their universities will not pay their expenses to these meetings.

The benefits of collaboration with school teachers may seem much more obvious to university faculty in those situations where they can work with local high school teachers and, in turn, accept students of those teachers into their own university classes. This is much more likely to happen in the case of public universities, since many private universities, especially the most selective, have relatively few students from their local area. Yet we see numerous examples of magnanimous efforts by college faculty from both private and public institutions in all parts of the country who work with schools for the benefit of the profession and of society at large. On the national level, this interaction can be seen at the annual Institute and Workshops of the American Classical League and at the special sessions of the Annual Meeting of the American Philological Association sponsored by the Association's Division of Education. Regional associations such as the CAMWS, the Classical Association of the Atlantic States (CAAS), and the Classical Association of New England (CANE) always have peda-gogical presentations alongside philological papers.

It is not surprising, in light of the continual demands on college faculty, that many do not find time to visit and cooperate with local school teachers of Latin; to attend meetings of state and regional organizations where they could meet still more school teachers; to offer special courses for teachers in the late afternoons or evenings; to speak at Junior Classical League (JCL) banquets or foreign language assemblies; to appear before a hostile school board and argue for the preservation of a desperate teacher's program. Lynne Cheney, the current Chairman of the National Endowment for the Humanities, urges colleges in their tenure deliberations to begin to honor the work that college professors do with the schools. Recent years have shown that many college-level classicists have come to realize that we are all in this endeavor together, and that we will sink or swim together. It remains for more administrators to follow this lead and Cheney's advice.

Chapter Six

Teachers and the Teaching of Latin

The State of the Profession: 1990

One of the strengths of Latin has always been the dedicated teachers who have passed on the tradition of the language from one generation of students to the next. These teachers have always believed that Latin is eminently worthwhile and will make a difference in the lives of their students. One legendary Latin teacher, Maureen O'Donnell, who believed in the value of her discipline, told her students, "I will have failed if you do not leave this class a better person." A profound sense of mission like this has been and continues to be an important factor in the survival and growth of Latin as a discipline.

The Shortage of Teachers

The most pressing problem that Latin as a discipline faces in elementary and secondary education is the insufficiency of numbers of Latin teachers in almost every area of the country. Robert Wilhelm has detailed the enormity of the problem and suggested some means of beginning to remedy it in a well-documented article, "The Shortage of High-School Latin Teachers," published in a book edited by Richard LaFleur, *The Teaching of Latin in American Schools: A Profession in Crisis* (Scholars Press, 1987, pp. 17-30). In the introduction to this book, LaFleur has written:

> As a consequence of this shortage, plans to open new Latin programs or to expand existing ones have again and again in recent years been curtailed or even abandoned. In numerous other instances, however, teachers lacking certification, or teachers certified in other areas but with some training in Latin—often only two or three courses, taken 10 or 20 years earlier, in college or even in high school— have been hired or reassigned to teach in these new or expanded programs; in cases too frequent to contemplate, teachers with no formal instruction in Latin at all are being sent into the classroom by desperate or overzealous principals. Under such circumstances—and the phenomenon is by no means limited, but is occurring in hundreds of classrooms and affecting thousands of high schoolers throughout America—the students, the teachers themselves, and ultimately the Classics profession as a whole will suffer. We dare not run the risk of creating a generation of poorly taught and uninspired Latin students (p. xv).

For those of us who are currently in the profession, remedying this shortage must be our foremost concern. One of the best ways to do this is to encourage any classics major with even a small interest in teaching and thus expedite the metamorphosis of student into teacher.

The Preparation of Latin Teachers

The Latin teachers of today (and, no doubt, of tomorrow) are coming to the profession not only from Latin undergraduate or graduate-school programs, but also from other various and sometimes surprising sources. Some have been teaching other subjects; some taught Latin before, but many years ago; some have never taught, but want to try it in their mature or retirement years. But whatever their past or point of entry, they need to be prepared for the task of teaching. The range of preparatory programs ranges from short refreshers to four- or five-year programs leading to certification and the Bachelor's or Master's degree.

Some Basic Tenets

There are several presumptions about the teaching and learning of Latin that underlie this report. They are as follows:

- Latin literature and documentary sources put teachers in direct contact with the Romans. A deepening acquaintance with texts in the original is crucial to their appreciation of Roman culture, history and language.

- The learning of grammar and reading of Latin passages should be integrated. From the very beginning of language study, the teacher should use various strategies to promote understanding of the Latin text. Translation should be only ONE of many ways of accomplishing this goal.

- In order to appreciate the nuances of Latin literature, a knowledge of Roman history (including art and architecture) and Roman culture (lifestyles, values) is essential.

- The oral component of Latin is an important means of deepening a teacher's understanding of the language and literature. Both teacher and students benefit from reading Latin aloud with the correct pronunciation and accentuation.

Undergraduate Preparation of Prospective Teachers

Colleges and universities can provide undergraduates with a good start to their teaching careers. First of all, students should acquire a solid grounding in Latin. Other aspects of their program can be arranged with a minimum of difficulty if they are well grounded in Latin. This requires a classics department in which all faculty members offer encouragement to prospective teachers; and secondly, one in which all members can offer practical guidance to these students so that they can become classroom teachers with the most efficient use of their preparation time.

Guidelines for an Undergraduate Program

In this section we will propose guidelines for students intending to teach Latin. The aim of these guidelines is to help undergraduates plan their program so they can best prepare themselves for a career in secondary teaching, and to offer post-secondary institutions a look at a general description of an ideal (but minimal) program. Much of the inspiration for this list comes from a document produced by Jon Mikalson and others at a conference funded by the Classics Project of the Center for the Liberal Arts at the University of Virginia. Since the training of teachers does not stop upon receipt of a degree but continues throughout a career, these guidelines will also serve as suggestions for topics for the continuing education of practicing teachers.

An Undergraduate Program for Latin Teachers

Latin (beyond the beginning sequence) . . . . .21 credits

Related courses . . . . .9 credits

A minor area of study in *either* education and pedagogy courses *or* a second content area (English, another language etc.). If a formal major is not possible, a student might organize a program using electives in classics available outside his or her non-classics major.

Suggested Topics in Latin

The following topics may be taught in a variety of course combinations and may require more than one semester to cover.

- Advanced grammar: review of grammar, characteristics of Latin prose style and poetic features

- Cicero: (1) oratory: the *First Catilinarian;* selections from the *Pro Caelio* etc.; (2) selected letters; (3) philosophy: *Somnium Scipionis* etc., including a discussion of prose style, politics of the late republic and the Roman philosophical tradition

- Vergil: *Aeneid,* Books I and IV, and selections from Books II and VI, including the Augustan context, analysis of poetic style and metrics

- Ovid: selections from the *Metamorphoses,* including the epic tradition, analysis of poetic style, Roman religion, Ovid's treatment of myth

- Historians: selections from Caesar, *De Bello Gallico,* Book I; *Bellum Civile,* Book I; Livy, *Ab Urbe Condita,* Book I; Sallust, *Catiline,* including politics of the late republic, Roman historiography

- Lyric poetry: selections from Catullus and Horace's *Odes,* including analysis of poetic style, Greek influence, metrics

- Oral Latin and sight reading: strategies for teaching the reading of Latin aloud and developing the speaking skill in the classroom; strategies for reading Latin passages for comprehension, analysis and appreciation

The above list is basic. More Latin should be read if time permits. Other authors could easily be included, as well as genres not listed above.

Supplements to a Bachelor's Program

Teacher candidates should choose, whenever possible, from among the following electives:

- Selections from Plautus and Terence
- Latin language and style
- Greek comedic tradition
- Roman theater and stagecraft
- Satire: selections from Horace, Juvenal and Petronius;
  Roman origins, private life, European satirical tradition
- Epistles: selections from Cicero, Seneca and Pliny;
  Roman private and political life, biography,
  epistolographic tradition, Stoicism
- History: selections from Tacitus
- selections from medieval Latin; Latinity, transmission of texts,
  Christian traditions
- Related courses (a choice of at least 3):

Roman History	Roman Art
Roman Civilization and Life	Classical Mythology
Roman Literature in Translation	

- Other useful courses:

Greek Literature in Translation	Classical Archaeology
Greek History	Greek
Greek Civilization	Ancient Philosophy
Greek Art	Historical Linguistics
A Romance Language	Etymology

Teacher Training: An Example of an Ideal M.A.T. Program

Although there are a number of programs that offer teacher training around the country, here the focus is on a very successful Master of Arts in Teaching (MAT) Latin and Classical Humanities program that has turned out dozens of teachers since its beginning in 1970. It is the MAT-Latin program at the University of Massachusetts at Amherst, and it can serve as a model for Latin teacher training elsewhere. This program is the result of a successful dialogue between the Department of Classics and the School of Education, and it is such cooperation that results in the success of a content-based teacher-training program, whether an MAT program like that at the University of Massachusetts or a five-year certificating program like those becoming standard at other universities.

In the course of the Massachusetts two-year program, students are required to take 25 credit hours of courses in the content area. In addition they must take13 graduate credits in education courses (two courses of this credit are in Latin pedagogy, taught by the Department of Classics with the approval of the Teacher Education Coordinating Council of the School of Education) and 9 credits of practice teaching. A special feature of the Latin pedagogy classes is that students have an opportunity to design, test out and evaluate their own teaching materials. Students are also strongly encouraged to bring or do an unofficial minor of at least 18 undergraduate credits in a modern foreign language or English in order to prepare for a second field of certification. In 1993, this program will be modified to offer provisional or permanent certification in Latin for middle- as well as high-school teachers.

The strengths of a program of this type are several: the program has a strong academic focus on Latin itself; the methodology courses are designed and taught by classics professors, separate from but supervised by the school of education; students have ample opportunity to obtain teaching experience, both in the high school classroom and also as teaching assistants in elementary and intermediate Latin courses at the university; the classics department enjoys good relationships with the school of education and thus students obtain teaching certificates along with the MAT-Latin degrees; and the classics department has a strong network with secondary teachers throughout the state. All of these features make this program an innovative and attractive model for other teacher-training programs.

There are some important lessons to be learned in general from the way the above program has been designed. One of these is the essential nature of the dialogue between classics departments, colleges, and state departments of education. When there is rivalry and dissension among these units, all groups suffer, but the ultimate losers are the student who fails to be trained adequately as a teacher and the profession at large that cannot find enough qualified teachers.

Another essential component of a succesful teacher-training program is the network developed by a classics department with Latin teachers and classical organizations around the state. This kind of collaboration promotes in students and faculty an awareness and an appreciation of school teaching in the "real world"; encourages the creation and dissemination of high quality teaching materials; aids candidates in finding student-teaching sites and permanent positions; and most important of all, creates an enduring support network to give help and encouragement to aspiring members of a profession where teachers are often isolated.

Teacher Certification: The M.Ed. Degree and the Holmes Report

In order to teach in the public schools, prospective teachers must fulfill certain requirements set by each state and be certified as competent to teach. Requirements usually include an undergraduate or graduate major in the content area (or a specified number of courses in the content area) as well as a designated number of hours of education courses (including a set number of hours in the classroom under observation and supervision). There are various routes by which a prospective teacher may complete these requirements but an increasingly common route is for the student to complete an undergraduate degree in the content area and then earn a Master of Education degree that provides courses in education and an opportunity for practice time in the classroom. This model, supported by the recent Holmes Report, ensures that prospective teachers study longer before they enter the classroom; however, it also proposes a serious threat to all MAT programs. The advantage of the MAT program for the training of Latin teachers is, of course, the continued emphasis on the study of Latin during the Master's program. The question of which of these models will prevail will be an important one for Latin-teacher education and will call for careful scrutiny in the next decade.

Students may also receive certification in a second teaching field. This requires a smaller number of courses in that discipline—usually around 20-30 semester credits. It is in the best interest of Latin teachers who wish to have full-time teaching assignments to become certified in a second field. This second area might be another language, but, if not, can be any other discipline in the secondary-school curriculum. High-school administrators are also often favorably disposed to candidates who are willing to coach a sport, sponsor a club or supervise other extracurricular activities.

Testing of Teacher Candidates

A number of states now require that new Latin teachers successfully complete a content area examination before they begin their teaching career. These examinations test for minimal proficiency in the content area, usually at the level of a first or second year Latin program. In some states (e.g. Florida) the examinations have been written by committees of teachers and college professors who follow a careful blueprint of specifications. The National Teachers Examination (NTE) division of the Educational Testing Service (ETS) has also recently prepared a Latin teachers' examination for seven states: Connecticut, Michigan, New York, North Carolina, South Carolina, Tennessee and Virginia. Candidates are tested in the areas of Latin language skills, Roman civilization, English word study, and pedagogical and professional knowledge. Since the clientele for this examination will have completed (or be completing) a Latin major, some education courses and a student teaching requirement, most candidates should not find difficulty with it. If this new NTE in Latin fulfills its three stated purposes—to measure competence, to provide quantitative information to certification boards, and to aid educational institutions in teacher preparation, we may see its use extended to many more states.

Alternative Routes to Certification

Because of the shortage of teachers in areas such as mathematics, foreign languages and the sciences, some states (e.g. New Jersey) have developed alternative certification programs that allow qualified individuals to teach in the classroom without having completed the education portion of the certification requirements. Alternative certification usually involves working with a master teacher during the first year of teaching, as well as completing a specified course of study during that year. Experience has shown that having a connection with a classics teacher/mentor is often the crucial element in the success of these new teachers.

In most states, certified teachers are also required to upgrade their certificates every several years. Latin teachers can do this by taking summer or evening courses in a classics department or in education, and by attending workshops and/or travel programs. Since the courses in Latin are usually the most crucial, it is incumbent upon college and university classics departments to provide these courses to teachers at times they can take them so that they can keep current with their discipline.

Criteria for the Certification of Teachers

Minimum standards for certification in Latin may be described in terms of the following competencies: language analysis, reading comprehension, culture and civilization, oral proficiency, and teaching methodology. The levels of competence presented here are appropriate for a beginning teacher. Such a teacher will be able to cope in Latin, Levels I and II, and may even have some familiarity with advanced knowledge and skills. In contrast one might expect that an experienced teacher would display greater breadth and depth of knowledge and skills, teach more advanced classes (such as Latin, Levels III, IV or V, and/or Advanced Placement courses), and demonstrate superior ability on teaching evaluations.

Competencies for the Beginning Latin Teacher

These are based in part on a document produced by a series of committees of high-school teachers and college faculty in the state of Florida who were involved in the writing of the Latin examination for initial certification.

- Language analysis: this competency demonstrates a knowledge of etymo-logical application, vocabulary in context, and grammar and syntax.

- Reading comprehension: this competency demonstrates an ability to read and understand a straightforward passage of connected Latin prose or poetry.

- Culture and civilization: this competency demonstrates a knowledge of classical mythology, Roman literary history, Roman political history, Roman social history, and an awareness of Roman contributions to Western civilization.

- Oral proficiency: this competency demonstrates an ability to read Latin aloud with accuracy and expression and to use spoken Latin at a basic level in the classroom setting.

- Teaching methodology: this competency demonstrates an ability to use appropriate techniques for teaching language analysis, reading comprehen-sion, culture and civilization, and oral proficiency.

The competencies defined above may be more precisely defined as a series of skills that are appropriate to a beginning teacher.

Professional Development

At a time when many Latin teachers are feeling isolated and increasingly pressured, one way in which teachers can find support is through participation in classical associations. In a number of states such as Florida, Texas and Virginia, state classical organizations are strong and offer an excellent means of making contacts and exchanging ideas. Teachers are also urged to join regional organizations such as the Classical Association of the Atlantic States, the Classical Association of the Middle West and South or the Classical Association of New England. All three of these regional organizations have made a strong commitment to supporting teachers in various ways: the CAAS provides helpful surveys of texbooks and audio-visual aids in its journal; the CANE offers a summer program, each year with a different theme, and a very helpful newsletter/journal; the CAMWS provides scholarships for participation in summer programs in Rome and Athens, as well as scholarships for entering freshmen who agree to take Latin in college. The CAMWS has also recently begun to provide small stipends to enable teachers to go to a CAMWS annual meeting for the first time and to help with tuition fees for those teachers working to become certified in Latin. Other state associations such as those in California, Colorado, Florida, Illinois, Louisiana, Massachusetts, New York, Texas and Virginia maintain an active schedule of meetings and activities.

Professional Organizations

In addition to their local and state associations, secondary-level teachers will especially want to join the American Classical League, a national organization that publishes two journals and a newsletter, and offers a wide variety of teaching materials through its Teaching Materials and Resource Center. The ACL also oversees the coordinating teachers' committee of the Junior Classical League, a large organization of high-school Latin students, whose main aim is the promotion of the study of the ancient world, and it operates a very successful Teacher Placement Service out of its office at Miami University, Oxford, Ohio. The ACL also sponsors the Senior Classical League on the college level and the Elementary Teachers of Classics and Classics Clubs at the elementary- and middle-school levels.

Teachers wishing to keep abreast of scholarship in the field of ancient history and classical philology should join the American Philological Association and/or the Archaeological Institute of America; teachers of Vergil should join the Vergilian Society of America, which publishes a yearly journal and sponsors, in the summers, study tours of Greek and Roman sites in the Mediterranean world. The Vergilian Society summer programs at the Villa Vergiliana, in Cuma, Italy, are especially geared to helping teachers of the *Aeneid*.

Summer Courses

Since many teachers in the public school system need to upgrade their teaching certificate every several years, a college course in the content area is most easily done in the summer, especially by those teachers who do not live near a university or college. Other teachers may feel the necessity of taking a refresher course before attempting to offer Advanced Placement courses. Information concerning courses and programs is available in the *Newsletter* of the American Classical League.

Ongoing Training: an Ideal Program

At Hunter College in New York City (and at S.U.N.Y. at Stonybrook in the summer), courses for experienced and new Latin teachers are offered on a year-round basis by classics faculty. Professor William Mayer and colleagues have developed a plan of offering courses for practicing and prospective secondary-level teachers that meet in the fall and spring semesters once a week for three hours when it is possible for secondary teachers to attend. The teachers analyze and discuss Latin texts which they are using or are planning to use in their classrooms. An important component of these classes is the development of classroom-ready materials for the teaching of the texts which are read in the courses. Teachers are given a voice concerning the time of class meetings, the selection of Latin texts and the types of materials to be produced.

Typical course offerings are Teaching Latin Prose (or Poetry) and Review of Latin Grammar (with emphasis on teaching grammar and on reading Latin aloud). Since each teacher in one of these courses creates a set of materials, all members come away with a full and varied packet of teaching materials that have been tried, critiqued and improved by peers. Teachers learn much from the professor and from each other in this format. An additional benefit in taking such courses is the New York State re-certification credit system that offers highly desirable incentives for this ongoing training. There is a gap—often quite wide—between being able to read a Latin text and being able to teach it. Taking a course given by an experienced classics teacher who is interested in both literature and pedagogy can help teachers bridge that gap.

NEH Summer Institutes in Teacher Preparation

The National Endowment for the Humanities has also made an effort to encourage teachers to return to the classroom in the summer as students with the expectation that teachers, once they are challenged and stimulated, will carry some of that excitement back to their classrooms. The New England Classical Institute at Tufts University, Medford, Massachusetts, which has a long history of providing summer enrichment for teachers, has recently received NEH funding to continue encouraging intellectual growth in teachers. In addition, the NEH has also made a special effort to assist in the training of new Latin teachers. It has recently funded programs at the University of Georgia, Athens, and Westminster College, New Wilmington, Pennsylvania, which were designed to train teachers certified in other subjects to become certified in Latin as well. Both of these programs have been very successful in providing the profession with additional Latin teachers in relatively short periods of time.

Summer Seminars

The NEH has also funded college faculty to provide summer seminars on a single author or a thematic approach. Classical authors studied range chronologically from Homer to Tacitus on a wide variety of themes. University professors from all parts of the country plan and teach these seminars which are offered at various colleges and universities. Teachers' expenses are paid and a stipend is offered for attending; they are welcomed as colleagues and scholars by college faculty. Both the professors and the participants unanimously assert that these seminars provide a stimulating and refreshing intellectual experience, and a perfect opportunity to meet new colleagues and mentors.

Opportunities for Foreign Travel

At some time in their teaching career all Latin teachers ought to have the opportunity to travel in Italy or Greece. The best way in which to get an orientation to the past is to attend the excellent summer programs provided by the American Academy in Rome or the American School of Classical Studies at Athens. The Vergilian Society of America offers a number of educational tours for classicists each summer to Italy, and to other sites in Africa, France, Germany, Spain, Turkey etc. There is nothing like a visit to ancient sites to quicken teachers' enthusiasm. After such an experience, some teachers also arrange to take some of their students for a quick tour of the high points of the classical world during spring vacation or in the summer.

Scholarships for Teachers

The best source of information about available scholarships is the local classical association. These organizations have lists of scholarships for summer programs abroad, such as those offered by the ACL, CAMWS, and some of the state classical organizations. Recently the Rockefeller Foundation and the Council for Basic Education began offering summer fellowships for teachers to study at the American Academy in Rome and the Vergilian Society's Villa Vergiliana in Cuma, Italy, or to plan their own independent program of study.

One Latin teacher, for example, was awarded a grant to travel along in the wake of Aeneas, as described in Vergil's *Aeneid*.

Latin Teaching Assignments: Some Realities

Since the resurgence of Latin in the late seventies, Latin programs have assumed an unprecedented variety of configurations. Many programs in public schools offer the possibility of teaching only the first two years of Latin, since enrollments do not warrant upper level classes. In such programs Latin teachers who want full-time employment must fill in their day by teaching another subject in the same school, or by serving as itinerant teachers in other district schools. It is not at all unusual for a Latin teacher to work at two or three different schools. Not all teachers dislike these arrangements, but most would prefer to teach in one school in order to establish closer working ties with their colleagues and to become a full member of their school community. There is also the practical concern of the time and effort of driving across a city or county in all kinds of weather and carting materials between buildings.

Mixed-Level Classrooms

If teachers are fortunate enough to teach in schools where upper levels of Latin are offered, they may be faced with mixed-level classes. Because of the generally smaller numbers of students who study Latin as opposed to modern languages, it is the norm rather than the exception to have Latin, Levels III and IV, taught in the same room during the same class period. Most teachers respond to this necessity by alternating their curricular offerings from one year to the next. In some instances, even more extreme examples of mixed levels are found, such as a Latin, Levels I and II, in combination, or worse, Latin, Levels II, III and IV, together. This practice is to be decried, and at best allowed only as an emergency remedy for a teacher shortage or temporarily low enrollments. A multilevel classroom can be a source of stress and frustration for both teachers and students.

Rushing into Advanced Placement Courses

Another consequence of administrators being forced to conform to preset numbers in the teacher/students ratio is the teaching in many schools of the Advanced Placement syllabus at the third-year level rather than in the fourth or fifth year. As a result of this situation, many students go directly from introductory grammar review into reading Vergil or Catullus or Horace with little experience in reading continuous Latin prose or poetry of any kind. Often these students are not adequately prepared for the rigorous work that the Advanced Placement syllabus requires. Teaching such unprepared students a demanding syllabus puts a special burden on a teacher. Problems also arise when teachers are not adequately prepared to teach what is effectively a college-level course.

Difficulty in Obtaining Materials

Another fact of life for a teacher in the public schools of some states is a cumbersome state or county process of approval and adoption of teaching materials. Where this exists, teachers have little flexibility in shaping their own curricula. A number of our survey respondents stated that they did not hesitate to spend their own money, or invent ingenious schemes, when budget constraints threatened to prevent them from examining and obtaining good innovative teaching materials.

Distance Learning

In this age of mass communication an exciting development in classroom teaching deserves mention, viz. the advent of the electronic classroom. In several states, notably Texas and Virginia, the video classroom is being employed to bring Latin instruction to several hundreds of students in far-flung rural areas. This kind of teaching obviously requires extensive preparation and lesson planning, and a certain amount of camera presence on the part of the teacher. Certainly any school district offering such classes should offer specialized training to the teacher who undertakes this completely new type of presentation. Another minor but growing trend in education is the "home classroom," where parents have secured permission from local authorities to teach their children at home. Latin is being studied at home through such programmed learning methods as Waldo Sweet's *Artes Latinae*. It is unlikely that this mini-trend will have any major impact on the national scene, but it is reassuring that the demand for Latin persists even in this alternative setting.

Teaching with the New Textbooks and Methods

The 1924 Report on the status of Latin called *The Classical Investigation* made the case that reading Latin, the "ability to read Latin as Latin, that is, to get hold of the sense in the Latin order without translation" (p. 189), is the primary objective in the study of Latin:

> The indispensable primary immediate objective in the study of Latin is progressive
> development of ability to read and understand Latin. . . . In the attainment of this
> primary immediate objective several secondary objectives are involved, such as the
> ability to pronounce Latin, sufficient knowledge of Latin vocabulary, syntax and
> forms, and the ability to translate Latin into English and English into Latin (p. 32).

Many of the texts used in American classrooms of the past few decades do not, however, appear to have the same laudable aim. A glance at the traditional textbooks used in many Latin classrooms reveals that learning vocabulary, forms and syntax are the immediate objectives of the course and that reading is considered the end product of the process, delayed in many cases until all the grammar has been "finished." The 1924 Report contends (as many Latin teachers believe), however, that the fact that a student has been introduced to all the rules of grammar and syntax does not necessarily mean that he or she can read or translate Latin.

The Reading Method Textbooks

Recent Latin pedagogy has again begun to emphasize the importance of reading as a goal in learning the language. Textbooks such as *Ecce Romani,* the *Cambridge Latin Course* and the *Oxford Latin Course* put considerable emphasis on the students' reading of a continuous Latin narrative from the very beginning. *The Oxford Latin Course,* for example, states the aim of its narrative as follows:

> When we say that the overriding aim of the course is to teach our pupils to read
> Latin fluently and intelligently, we mean ideally that we want them to understand
> Latin as they read it without translating. Translation is the traditional and the most

precise method of testing understanding. Teachers will certainly use it for much of the time, but ... it is highly desirable to vary the reading lesson by sometimes asking comprehension questions instead of demanding a full translation. The ultimate test of understanding the sense of a passage is for the teacher to read it aloud in Latin while the pupils do not look at the text and then test their understanding by reading-comprehension questions or by asking them to retell the story in their own words in English (*Teacher's Book,* pp.10-11).

Inductive Teaching

These same textbooks also rely on the teacher's use of the inductive method of teaching, i.e. helping the students to infer the grammatical principles, syntax and meanings, rather than presenting the elements of a system as something to be memorized and then applied. But there can be no doubt that a method of teaching that emphasizes reading as the immediate goal and uses the inductive method to achieve that goal provides a considerable challenge to Latin teachers. It is far simpler to transmit a ready made, memorizable set of principles to students than to help them learn to understand Latin more as the Romans did. Hence these new pedagogical methods have made teaching Latin a demanding and far-from-routine task.

Many school districts offer their teachers special workshops in how to teach reading skills to their students from the very beginning of Latin, Level I. Our profession can benefit from the considerable body of pedagogical work on the teaching of reading in English and the modern foreign languages. In the future we can expect to hear more about the various levels of reading and the mechanisms that readers employ in any language to read at different levels of proficiency. The strategies needed in reading a Latin passage can be described and taught just as is done in the teaching of reading English or any other native language.

Conclusion

Until the problem of the teacher shortage is solved, Latin programs in secondary schools continue to be in jeopardy. The teacher shortage does not have a simple solution, but is a problem that must be attacked in a number of different ways: meaningful communication and interaction between classics departments and teachers in secondary-level programs; more innovative teacher training programs; expanded opportunities for teachers to engage in professional development; and continued innovation in the high school Latin curriculum. Prospective Latin teachers come to their programs with enthusiasm and willingness; it is essential that they be properly welcomed into the profession, encouraged, and provided with the knowledge and tools that help them become the best possible teachers. The future of the classics profession depends on them.

Chapter Seven

Brief Overviews of Latin Study in Canada and Britain

Canada

High-school Latin programs in Canada are clustered primarily in southern Ontario, in Ottawa and Montréal; and in and around Victoria and Vancouver. Latin programs are also found here and there in other provinces, but these represent a very small proportion of the total enrollment. In Ontario, there were some 8,000 high-school Latin students in 1988, down nearly 20% from the enrollment in 1985, and 50% from the enrollment in 1973.

Since Canada is officially bilingual (English and French) and also has a large multicultural population, Latin has had to compete (even more intensely than in the United States) for breathing space in the crowded high-school foreign language curriculum. In 1985, in Ontario, province-wide curricular changes effectively reduced the length of the average Latin program to three years, thereby forcing many Latin teachers to compress, with varying degrees of success, their five year programs into three, with the third year reserved for the new Ontario equivalent of the U.S. College Board Advanced Placement credits, called "Ontario Academic Credits (OAC)." The OAC offer study in a syllabus of readings around Latin genres or themes such as Love and Friendship, Urban Planning etc.

The OAC syllabus, organized as it is around themes of contemporary interest, deserves wider attention and emulation elsewhere in Canada and in the United States as a possible solution to the narrowed time frame into which Latin study has been relegated by the emphases on mathematics, computer studies, science and the so-called critical modern foreign languages. The response to this curricular squeeze, which has been keenly felt in Canada, in Britain and the United States, has taken two basic forms: teach more Latin in less time, progressing quickly through the grammar to as many different Latin authors as possible; or teach only those rudiments of the Latin language and culture that contribute more or less directly to the understanding of the English language and western civilization. Since time is limited in either case, the interest and ability of the students dictates to a large extent which option a given school system chooses.

England and Wales

In 1988 the British government passed a sweeping new Education Act, establishing, *inter alia,* a National Curriculum for all students in state schools aged 5-16. (Private schools are not required to adopt the National Curriculum but are encouraged to give it their attention.) Under this Act, some 90% of the curriculum is to be devoted to ten legally obligatory core and foundation subjects. Latin, however, is not included in these subjects and thus will have to compete with other subjects not included in the National Curriculum for any remaining time. Thus Latin is more vulnerable than ever before, particularly since there is no legal restraint on a given school to devote 100% of its curriculum to the ten core and foundation subjects. (In practice this is thought unlikely to happen.) Also, financial considerations may not allow the hiring of staff for minority subjects outside the National Curriculum. Classical humanities, called in Britain "classical studies," are similarly threatened, though the final report of the History Working Group does contain study units on ancient Greece and the Roman empire.

Mr. Kenneth Baker, formerly Secretary of State for Education and Science, has responded to critics of the new National Curriculum declaring that Latin and classical humanities should not be viewed narrowly as separate subjects but as interdisciplinary. Classical humanities have been preserved in the curriculum, according to Mr. Baker, by incorporating them into the ten core and foundation subjects. Accordingly, he has asked the National Curriculum Groups on English and History to "consider the contribution of classical studies, as a cross-curricular theme, to the attainment targets and programmes of study for these subjects" (*J.A.C.T. Review,* Second Series, Number 5, Summer 1989, p.2). As for Latin, Mr. Baker argues that "most" people would argue that "Latin should be available as an option for the more able pupils" (ibid.), i.e. the minority of students who go on to the "sixth form" when aged 17-18, or, in American terms, those who study college preparatory subjects.

The recent modification in the National Curriculum, announced in January 1991 by Mr. Kenneth Clarke, then Secretary of State for Education, requires the new mandated curriculum only of children up to age 14 (not up to age 16, as previously). This change will facilitate the retention of Latin and Classics in the more open curriculum for children aged 14-16.

Events in Britain show vividly how vulnerable teachers of Latin can be to centralized decisions about the curriculum. Although there are disadvantages to the American policy of local control of schools (e.g. Philistinism among school board members or inadequate funding), it does provide safety against peremptory across-the-board decisions at the federal level and guarantees the possibility of citizen input and local choice. The establishment in 1989, by U.S. President George Bush, of the National Education Goals Panel may lead to the establishment in the 1990's of a national curriculum for the U.S. If so, American teachers of Latin may be forced as are their British colleagues to assure a place for their subject in a nationally prescribed curriculum. The only subjects mentioned *by name* in the NEG Panel's published goals are English, mathematics, science, history and geography, but one of the NEG Panel's announced objectives is to foster the increase of the "percentage of students who are competent in more than one language" (NEG Panel, *Compendium of Interim Resource Group Reports* (March 25, 1991), p. 37).

Chapter Eight
Brief Overview of the Teaching of Greek in the U.S.

In 1986, the college-level enrollment in ancient Greek was 17,608, down by 9% from the 1983 enrollment of 19,350 (*ADFL Bulletin*, 19.2 (January 1988) 41). The public high-school enrollment in 1985 was 354 in ancient Greek, and 487 in modern Greek (*Foreign Language Annals*, 20 (October 1987) 469). The figure for high-school enrollment in private schools is not available, but the number of students, in 1990, participating in the National Greek Examination, which included both public and private schools (and a small number of college level students), was 779. A reasonable estimate of the total number of high-school age students currently studying ancient Greek in the United States is 800.

A 1990 survey by the National Greek Examination of the ancient Greek textbooks used at the high-school level shows surprising variety. With 45 high schools reporting, 12 use the J.A.C.T.'s *Reading Greek;* 7, Crosby and Schaeffer's *An Introduction to Greek;* 6, Schoder and Horrigan, *A Reading Course in Homeric Greek;* 4, Chase and Phillips, *New Introduction to Greek.* The remaining 16 schools use 10 different textbooks. Of these, only Schoder & Horrigan's was written primarily for the high-school level, and it is used almost exclusively in Roman Catholic schools. Very recently a British school textbook, *Athenaze,* has been revised by Balme & Lawall and distributed in North America by the Oxford University Press.

Besides the scarcity of textbooks written for this level, high school teachers of ancient Greek are faced with a constricted schedule that leaves little time for Greek; a tiny minority of students interested; and little, if any, articulation between school and college-level programs. Most departments of Classics assume that their majors will begin Greek at the college level.

Chapter Nine

Recommendations for the Teaching of Latin

1. In an age when the need to communicate effectively is critical, all students can benefit from the study of Latin. We must take them all with whatever deficiencies they may have, and try to structure programs that offer the best opportunity for some degree of success to every student. This includes many groups that have not traditionally studied Latin: "Limited English Proficiency" students, Learning Disabled students, the economically and culturally disadvantaged, the handicapped, and students "at-risk."

2. Since teachers are dealing with a wider range of academic readiness and ability in today's Latin student, they must begin by teaching basic tasks, information and concepts. Students need to be taught how to study; how to do homework; how to organize their work and their thinking; what nouns and verbs are; what a sentence is; where Greece and Rome are. These "basics" can be an invaluable contribution to the lives of some students who may not, alas, learn them elsewhere and, of course, they are the *sine qua non* for further success in Latin.

3. The objectives for Latin programs should be expanded from learning grammar and translation to include a focus on lifelong educational benefits to be gained. Students of Latin should develop an elementary awareness of how languages work; how they are similar and how they differ; how English and the Romance languages are indebted to Latin; how our American experience was shaped and continues to be influenced by the ancient Greeks and Romans.

4. The improvement of English language skills is a major objective and result of Latin study. Our Latin courses should include a strong component of etymology and English vocabulary work. Knowledge about English grammar, sentence structure and style should be among the outcomes of Latin study.

5. Continued forceful efforts must be made to bring about collaboration among the different levels of Latin teaching. Elementary-, middle- and

high-school teachers, teachers at community colleges and university professors can and must work together. Collaborative efforts produce the energy, diversity and new life of our profession.

6. The modern foreign languages have much to offer Latin teachers. Besides legislative and financial benefits from being included under the rubric of "foreign language study," they benefit from their research, pedagogical programs and advocacy power. Latin teachers should actively pursue closer connections with modern foreign language associations.

7. All teachers of Latin should feel encouraged to employ some flexibility and variety in their teaching. The traditional stereotype of the quiet, predictable, teacher-centered classroom can be expanded to include active student involvement in learning, interaction between students, oral work for every student every day and strategies to accommodate differing learning styles. Successful programs give each student a sense of being an appreciated member of a team united by the common goal of studying the classics.

8. All students should have instruction and practice in the pronunciation, reading aloud and recitation of Latin. This not only facilitates comprehension and memorization, but enhances students' appreciation of Latin as a language. The prospect of studying Latin as a language that was spoken for hundreds of years is clearly more exciting than the mechanical deciphering of a mysterious code.

9. No one ever "finishes the grammar." The teaching of reading strategies and the systematic review of grammar should be continued at every level of Latin study. The overall design of the Latin program should be a spiral in which reading and consolidation of linguistic concepts reinforce each other each step of the way. The reading of meaningful and worthwhile material in Latin should begin as soon as possible, with the eventual goal of reading the Latin classics.

10. At the end of their Latin studies, even if these last only one year, students should begin to understand and appreciate the scope of classical studies: the languages and literature, the history and culture, and the substantial contributions of the ancient classical world to our own.

Chapter Ten

Brief Introduction to the Guidelines

The Need for the Guidelines

In response to the survey, many teachers indicated that they wanted a set of guidelines for Latin, Levels I and II, to get an idea of what is prescribed across the country, and to use as a touchstone for their own programs. As the NLG sub-committee set out to write these guidelines, it became obvious that such guidelines exist in abundance and are easy to obtain from numerous sources. Most states and counties have Standards of Learning guidelines; every textbook series offers a program overview and learning outcomes for each level; the five-level syllabus of the ACL/NJCL National Latin Exam is widely distributed and used. In addition, many Latin teachers meet together in their individual school districts to set their own curriculum guidelines.

This "one more" list, however, will offer at least a few new thoughts about progression, pace and emphasis, and may help some Latin teachers plan and evaluate their programs. Some will find the guidelines too general, but it should be remembered that they are offered as exactly that, general guidelines. Each teacher will be the best judge of what his or her program can accomplish at each level, given the resources, students and conditions of that particular situation, and given the constraints imposed by the programmatic goals of the various textbooks.

Overview of Survey Results

In broad terms, the survey results of the questions dealing with the level of presentation of grammatical topics may be summarized by the following statements:

- The great majority of Latin programs in the U. S. cover the bulk of Latin grammar in two years of high school study (or two semesters of college study).

- The chief differences between programs with regard to what is covered in Latin, Level I, as opposed to Latin, Level II, arise from the differences in textbooks.

- Some teachers choose to move at a somewhat slower pace (for a variety of reasons, e.g. need more review time, have fewer meetings per week, wish to teach more ancillary material, prefer a less hurried atmosphere in classes).

- Some teachers (10%-25%, depending on item) reported that they teach irregular verbs, deponent verbs, subjunctive uses and passive periphrastic constructions in the third year (or third semester of college).

- Continuous review of previously taught material was suggested by teachers at every level.

Chapter Eleven

Guidelines For
Latin, Levels I & II

1. The important thing for the teacher is not to complete a pre-set timetable, but to be sure the forms and their uses, in whatever order they may be presented in a given textbook, are understood, practiced and reviewed. If a program allows students to proceed at a quicker pace than the one suggested in these Guidelines, so much the better—as long as the majority of students are mastering the material.

2. The list of forms and constructions in the guidelines can be learned at several levels. Let us consider, for example, the ablative of means. Seeing it for the first time in a sentence or story, students might well translate it correctly. After an explanation, they might know the name of the construction; with further explanation (comparing it to other ablative uses), they might be able to describe the components of the construction and how it works. Finally (but not necessarily in this order), they might be able to write examples of it, or fill in a missing part in Latin. Generally, students solidify their understanding of given grammatical constructions over a period of time by meeting them repeatedly in the context of reading, by practice exercises, and by regular review. Therefore, it is assumed that students will be introduced to the forms and constructions listed in the Guidelines in either their first or second year, but may not completely master them until later.

Latin I (High School)
1st Semester (College)

Reading

Students can read simple narratives and dialogues in simple (made-up/adapted) Latin and easy (and/or highly annotated) original Latin texts. They can gather information from the Latin text, answer questions (in English) about content, paraphrase and translate it, and formulate judgments about its content. Students have regular practice at sight-reading and develop strategies for understanding sight readings. The quantity of reading will vary with age of students and availability of time.

Oral/Aural Skills

Students can pronounce the sounds of Latin, read simple sentences aloud with expression and generally correct pronunciation. Students can respond in Latin to simple Latin questions and can comprehend and write spoken Latin words, phrases and short sentences correctly. Teachers may wish to encourage oral skills by the use of games, skits, storytelling and other oral classroom activities.

Grammatical Concepts

Students understand the concept of inflection and the basic uses of the six cases of Latin (nominative, vocative, genitive, dative, accusative and ablative). They can recognize and describe the following basic grammatical concepts (Those marked with an asterisk are sometimes taught in the second year/semester.):

parts of speech	singular, plural
no article in Latin	gender
sentence	person
subject	tense
direct object	subject/verb agreement
indirect object	noun/adjective agreement
object of a preposition	infinitive vs. finite verb
direct address	auxiliary verb
predicate nominative, adjective	linking verb
possessive	principal parts as verb stems
declension	imperative
inflection	conjugation
base of Latin noun	active and passive* voice

Morphology

The forms below are usually learned during the first year (first semester of college) of Latin study. (The inclusion or exclusion of vocabulary items marked with a double asterisk** will depend on which textbook used.)

NOUNS: Six Cases	*PRONOUNS*
First Declension	ego, tu
Second Declension	is, ea, id
Third Declension	quis, quid
*Fourth Declension	qui, quae, quod
*Fifth Declension	*hic, haec, hoc
	*ille, illa, illud
	*idem, eadem, idem
	*ipse, ipsa, ipsum
	*sui, sibi, se, se

ADJECTIVES
First & Second Declension

Inter-declensional adjective/noun agreement
Possessives: meus, tuus, noster, vester
*Third Declension
*Comparative & Superlative Forms

ADVERBS
Interrogatives**: ubi, cur, quando, quomodo, quo, unde
Basic vocabulary list of adverbs**: bene, non, semper, olim,
        numquam, saepe, diu, valde, cras
Formation from First & Second Declension Adjectives
 *Formation from Third Declension Adjectives

PREPOSITIONS
ab, de, ex, sine, sub, cum, in, pro w/ablative
in, ad, per, contra, trans, circum, ob, propter (et al.**) w/accusative

CONJUNCTIONS
et, sed, aut, quod, nam, autem, ubi, -que, neque, atque, et al.**

INTERJECTIONS
O! Io! Eheu! Euge! Mehercle! etc.**

VERBS
Finite Forms: First-Fourth Conjugations:
        present, imperfect, future, perfect
        *past perfect, *future perfect—active & *passive voices
Imperatives: regular forms, singular & plural, active voice
        *duc, dic, fac, fer
Infinitives: present active, *present passive
Participles: perfect passive, *present active, *future active
Irregular verbs: sum, possum, *volo, *nolo, *fero, *eo

Syntax

The following grammatical constructions are usually taught during First Year Latin (first semester of college):

                nominative case as subject
                nominative case with linking verbs
                genitive case indicating possession
                dative case as indirect object
                *dative case w/ special adjectives
                accusative case as direct object
                accusative case as object of preposition
                place to which
                ablative case as object of preposition
                ablative of accompaniment

ablative of means
ablative of manner
ablative of time when
*ablative of agent
*ablative absolute
vocative case for direct address
*appositive
relative clause

* May be taught in second year/semester

Vocabulary

List depends on textbook. Students also learn Latin vocabulary through English derivatives, and vice versa.

Etymology

Students learn a brief history of the Latin language and begin to understand the linguistic and historical relationship between English and Latin. They have some practice using a Latin dictionary and a good English dictionary. Students can break down polysyllabic Latin derivatives into prefixes, roots and suffixes. They can recognize prefixes that have undergone spelling changes as a result of assimilation. Students know the meanings of all common Latin prefixes, suffixes and roots, and can use this knowledge to figure out the meanings of English words. They have a rudimentary understanding of the basic principles of word formation in Latin (e.g. *amo, amor, amator, amicus, amicitia, amabilis, amabilitas)* and how these correspond to parts of speech and meanings of English equivalents.

Roman Topics

Students learn about Roman family life, homes, clothing, the alphabet, schools and the city of Rome. They are introduced to the periods of Roman history, legendary heroes, geography of the Mediterranean, and the Greek and Roman gods and mythological stories. As they learn facts concerning these topics, they can make comparisons with their own culture and draw conclusions about the Romans. They are encouraged to consider the Roman influence on American life in the areas of language, government, architecture and ideas.

Latin II (High School)
2nd Semester (College)

Reading

Students can read longer passages in adapted Latin and they begin regular reading of original Latin texts. They can glean information from the Latin text, answer questions (in English) about content, paraphrase and translate it, make inferences and formulate judgments about its content. Students continue to have regular practice at sight-reading and developing strategies for understanding unseen readings.

Oral/Aural Skills

Practice in listening and reading aloud continues. Students learn to use reading aloud to help them understand the meaning of Latin. They learn to read with expression by breaking sentences into phrases according to meaning. Students can respond in Latin to simple Latin questions and can comprehend and write spoken Latin words, phrases, and short sentences correctly. Further oral activities such as skits, storytelling, question-and-answer drills, oral games, songs, and recitation performances are employed according to the predilection of the teacher.

Grammatical Concepts

Students continue their work on the uses of the six cases of Latin and the Latin verb system. They regularly review the basic grammatical concepts that they have previously learned and are introduced to the following:

> phrase vs. clause
> independent vs. dependent clauses
> adverbial, adjectival and noun clauses
> infinitives as nouns
> transitive vs. intransitive verbs
> irregular and defective verbs
> deponent verbs
> participles as adjectives
> direct vs. indirect statements
> direct vs. indirect questions
> direct vs. indirect commands
> *wish
> *condition
> indicative vs. subjunctive
> sequence of tenses
> enclitics
> substantive use of adjectives
> appositives
> prepositional phrases modifying verbs (not nouns)
> *gerund, gerundive
> idioms

* May be taught in third year/semester.

Morphology

The forms below are usually learned during the second year of Latin study (second semester of college Latin).

NOUNS:
locatives
irregular nouns or pronouns such as *vis, Iuppiter, nemo*

ADJECTIVES and PRONOUNS
uter, neuter, unus, solus, nullus, alter, ullus, totus, alius
quidam, aliquis, quisque, quisquam

ADJECTIVES	ADVERBS	QUESTION WORDS
irregulars	irregulars	
talis, qualis	eo, tam, ita	num, nonne
tantus, quantus		

VERBS
Imperatives: negatives, deponents
Infinitives: perfect active and passive, future active
Infinitive as verb in Indirect Statement
Irregular/defective verbs: fio, coepi, memini, odi, inquit
*Gerundive
Deponent verbs
Impersonal verbs: licet, oportet et al.
Subjunctive forms and uses:
    hortatory, jussive, purpose, result,
    indirect question/command, *cum*-temporal clauses
    *conditions, *anticipatory, *clauses of characteristic,
    *wishes, *deliberative subjunctive

* May be taught in third year/semester.

Syntax

The following grammatical constructions are usually taught during the second year (second semester of college Latin):

> genitive of the whole
> *dative of agent w/gerundive
> dative of purpose
> dative of possession
> dative w/compound verbs
> accusative case as subject of indirect statement
> accusative of extent, duration
> ablative of separation
> ablative of comparison
> ablative as object of *utor, fruor, vescor, potior, fungor*
> ablative of respect
> ablative of cause
> ablative of degree of difference
> relative purpose clause
> connecting relative

Vocabulary

List depends on texts read. Students also learn Latin vocabulary through English derivatives, and vice versa.

Etymology

Students continue to learn about the history of the Latin language and see the linguistic and historical relationship between Latin/English and Latin/Romance Languages . They contine to improve dictionary skills. Students continue the study of Latin derivatives in English and Latin word formation, extending their knowledge of prefixes, roots and suffixes.

Roman topics

Students deepen their knowledge of Roman customs and begin to acquire an overview of the periods of Roman history and literature. They become familiar with such historical figures as Caesar, Augustus, Hannibal, Cicero, and Vergil. They are introduced to Roman government and Rome's place in European history. The study of mythology continues, embracing the Olympians, the heroes and stories of Greek and Roman mythology. As students learn facts concerning these topics, they can make comparisons with their own culture and draw conclusions about the Romans. They are encouraged to continue and deepen their understanding of the Roman influence on American life in the areas of language, government, architecture and ideas.

Chapter Twelve

Concluding Observations

Some Reasons Why the Study of Latin is Useful for All American Students:

- The study of Latin offers a unique opportunity to look at the nature of language itself. A conscious study of Latin grammatical principles and accompanying traditional terminology (at appropriate maturity levels) will benefit students in their speaking and writing of English and in any further language study that they may undertake.

- The study of Latin can result in the broadening and deepening of students' English vocabulary and can impart an understanding of word formation, a most useful tool in approaching unfamiliar words.

- Latin is an excellent basis for the study of many modern languages, especially the Romance languages.

- On an elementary level, Latin can be very helpful in improving the English reading skills of students. Because it is a phonetic language, its study, especially practice in reading aloud, often brings to students the basic understanding of the phonetic principles that they may never have mastered when first learning to read English.

- When students study Latin, they enter the world of an alien (and for the most part ethnically neutral) culture, in some ways quite different from ours. Studying the language, customs, and world view of a society from a different time and place is a mind-expanding experience. Conversely, focusing on the similarities between our culture and that of the Romans offers the opportunity to consider the Graeco-Roman contribution to American life in the areas of government, architecture, ideals and ideas.

- The classics of Latin literature have had a significant influence on European, English and American literature and are eminently worth reading for themselves.

Some Truths about Latin Study:

- It is not necessary or advisable to complete the formal study of Latin grammar before being introduced to Latin literature. It is better to proceed to the reading of Latin as soon as possible, teaching supporting grammar while reading.

- Teachers' reports of the linguistic and grammatical readiness of today's students suggest that is is safest to expect that we will have to explain and teach some—or perhaps all—of the basic linguistic concepts that underlie the learning of Latin. Knowledge of these is often assumed by our textbooks, leaving materials and strategies for this entirely to teachers. These basic concepts such as noun, subject, sentence, part of speech, direct object etc., can be learned in small, palatable doses (based on the maturity of the student) along with learning to read and understand Latin.

- Latin should be used for meaningful communication as soon as possible in the course of instruction. The content and style of the reading material and exercises is important from the beginning. Reading Latin (as with any language) should be a means to an end, not only an end in itself. Students should glean information and experience enjoyment from their reading, not only derive satisfaction from deciphering a linguistic puzzle.

- Today's students have a lively curiosity about the Romans as people—their customs, their beliefs, and the way they lived their daily lives. Integrating material of this kind into Latin programs heightens students' interest in the Latin language.

- Since such an overwhelming percentage of students in Latin courses today list the improvement of verbal skills in English as a primary reason for their choosing Latin, teachers should consciously devote a certain amount of time to etymology and the principles of word formation, roots, prefixes and suffixes, working both from Latin to English and vice versa.

The Debate

The wide differences in emphasis among the methodologies in use today in Latin teaching suggest a certain vitality, even a ferment in the profession. It seems that teachers are poised somewhere between the old grammar translation method *(teach the grammar first, let them learn it by heart, then let them use it to read)* and the reading approach *(begin by reading lots of Latin stories that teach about the Romans; then let them learn the paradigms and construction names after they've seen them again and again in stories)*. Research in learning styles and second-language acquisition suggests that the best teaching method must combine these two approaches. The debate between the proponents of these two approaches will probably not be settled in favor of one method over the other: it is more likely that in the next decades an accommodation of both approaches will be accomplished by classroom teachers in conjuction with the developers of teaching materials.

The Traditional Model

The "Old Model" for the teaching of Latin in America dates back to the founding of this country and is based on a European model hundreds of years older. Simply described, the model prescribes that select fourteen year olds study Latin for two or three years. In the first year, they learn the declensions and conjugations; in the second year, they learn the syntactical constructions needed to read literature; in the third, they read (with painstaking struggle) a classic (Cicero's *Catilinarians* or Vergil's *Aeneid*). Although we have seen many variations and modifications of this, it remains the operating model for the teaching of Latin today.

The Pressures

If we want to see Latin survive and thrive, we must improve on this model and redefine it for American students today. In many of today's schools Latin is being taught exactly the way the teacher learned it—and the way his or her teacher learned it before. Judging from the responses to our survey, teaching today's student with yesterday's expectations is producing dark nights of self-doubt and frustration in great numbers of Latin teachers. When the teacher is feeling this kind of stress, it is very likely to trickle down to the student level. Worrying about county and state guidelines, state and national tests, what chapter will be finished by June, and how many lines of the *Aeneid* are read each day may prevent a teacher from creating a positive and reinforcing atmosphere in the classroom, and from accepting and enjoying the students for themselves. Students will enjoy their Latin classes if their teachers do, and will choose to take a second year, and a third and a fourth; they will spread the word that Latin is worthwhile and enjoyable.

The Pleasures of Learning

Certainly, it is possible that learning Latin can be an exciting activity in itself. Why is it that in all the surveys and questionnaires, the fourth, fifth and sixth grade students who are studying Latin always say they love it? Is it because the teachers of these younger students, sensing that they are embarking on a venture that is new, different and exciting, are willing to approach it in a new, different and exciting way? Is it perhaps that they have fewer preconceived notions about curriculum and pace, but more interest in the child and his or her response? All teachers will have their own peculiar strengths, weaknesses, enthusiasms, and particular style of their own. Let us remember that this is true also for older students.

Variety: More Chance for Student Success

Since there are endless ways of presenting the elements of the Latin language to students, teachers should build an arsenal of the newest, the oldest, and all kinds of proven and experimental techniques to choose from in the classroom each day. The use of a variety of techniques—including oral activities, group translation, rapid sight-reading, skits, oral reports, murals, competitions—not only injects life into Latin classrooms, but provides the best odds that every student will find a way to learn which works for him or her.

What to Read

Very few of the students who take Latin will major in it, and in fact, only about a quarter of the students who take Latin, Level I, in high school will take Latin, Level IV. Teachers need to make a serious examination of the choice of textbooks they present to their classes. Both high school and college teachers have been thinking for some time that the traditional Latin triad of Caesar, Cicero and Vergil is no longer appropriate—at least not in the same format in which it was presented in previous decades. Younger students seem to prefer reading works, or parts of works, which do not take an entire year to finish; they like to read about topics that are important to their age group, such as friendship, family, coming of age, comedy, love and adventure. College students may be more interested in history, politics and legal matters at this time of their life, but many also prefer the topics listed above.

The Role of Discussion in the Latin Classroom

What appeals to this generation are units based on themes, texts with a running vocabulary, with notes that are quickly available and easily understood, and readings that contain serious ideas that they can discuss with their teachers and classmates. They want to know the historical and cultural background of the texts they read, and the human stories that went into their making. When students become involved in the discussion of texts, recitation is replaced by analysis and opinion and learning becomes active rather than passive. This kind of personal interaction with fellow students and teachers creates the camaraderie that students crave and need. The Latin classroom becomes not just a daily stop-off place, but rather a place to exchange ideas and learn from others in a supportive, friendly and lively atmosphere.

A Fresh Look at our Goals

In 1924, *The Classical Investigation,* the major report on the teaching of Latin in this country sponsored by the American Classical League, proclaimed the goal of teaching Latin to be the ability to read Latin writers. In his article in *Helios* (Fall, 1987, p. 7-16), "The History of Latin Education," Professor George Kennedy of the University of North Carolina suggests that this may be an unattainable goal. He does not argue against the reading of classical texts, but rather suggests that it not be our primary goal in teaching the average student who enrolls in a Latin course. Most students do not learn Latin well enough in two years (or two college semesters)—or four—to read Latin authors with facility; to accomplish this takes years of study. Kennedy states (p.15) that "perhaps the major function of learning and teaching Latin in contemporary education should be as an introduction to the nature of language, to concepts of grammar, to etymology, and to cultural concepts conveyed through words."

Yet there are texts—inscriptions, proverbs, stories, poems—which students can read from the beginning of their Latin study, which enable them to establish direct communication with the ancient Romans. Today's Latin teacher can make use of these texts to help students, step by step, to achieve some proficiency in reading. The texts serve as the foundation of our courses, and it is from this base that we proceed to the "expanded goals": concepts of language, grammar, etymology and culture. Thus the Latin texts themselves—and our diverse ways of approaching them—form the basis for a substantial and practical program of instruction for today's Latin students.

Conclusion

In American education, Latin as a school subject seems to mean number of different things. Indeed it is a "package," an area study. It can improve academic performance in a variety of ways; students can learn solid, old-fashioned grammar and be exposed to great writing; they can learn some history, geography, philosophy, mythology and literary criticism. The fact that Latin study encompasses such a wide range of emphases and goals accounts for its surprising survival and liveliness in America today. We must not lose sight, however, of the fact that the teaching of the language itself and the reading of Latin texts remain the foundation and the *raison d'être* of our profession. We must continually re-examine and refine the traditional model to accommodate it to the needs of today's students. Many describe Latin study as an excellent vehicle for achieving a number of other instructional goals, as indeed it is; in the longer view, however, these "other goals" come and go, while the Latin itself remains.

Appendices

A. An "Ideal" Pre-College Latin Curriculum

This description of an ideal scope and sequence for Latin is offered in the following spirit: although none of us is fortunate enough to teach in a utopia where this curriculum exists, it can give us something to aim at! Also, it might serve as a help to those who are looking at an overall program that extends over more than one level (such as middle school and high school) while examining the articulation between the separate levels. In most real life cases, all the activities listed in grades four to nine are done in grade nine and many of our students do not begin Latin until tenth grade or later. This is presented as "food for thought" for teachers, parents, administrators and curriculum planners.

12th grade: . . . . *Latin V* . . . . *Advanced*

Literature—Lyric Poetry—Catullus/Horace (A.P. Syllabus)
          1-9 as in 11th grade (below)

11th grade: . . . . *Latin IV* . . . . *Advanced*

Literature—Epic Poetry—Vergil's Aeneid (A.P. Syllabus)
1. reading a substantial amount of authentic Latin literature
        (75 lines or more per week)
2. grammatical analysis
3. literary analysis (figures of speech, structure, theme)
4. historical, literary and philosophical background
5. producing an accurate and elegant (?) translation
6. metrics and scansion
7. participation in oral literary discussion
8. writing of critical essays
9. continued practice in reading aloud, especially poetry

10th grade: . . . . *Latin III* . . . . *Intermediate*
-continued practice in listening and reading aloud
-reading works or excerpts from several Latin prose authors
        (e.g. Pliny, Caesar, Cicero)
-review of grammatical structures and teaching of remaining structures
        (e.g. conditions, correlatives, future imperative et al.)
-investigation of Roman topics through readings in English
        (perhaps one each quarter), e.g. the Iliad, the Gallic Wars,
        the Hercules myth in the 20th century, the Roman city...

9th grade: . . . . *Latin II* . . . . *Intermediate*
-continued practice in listening and reading aloud
-continued reading of stories, dialogues, simplified and real Latin texts
-finish presentation of basic grammatical structures
        (uses of subjunctive, deponent verbs, indirect statment etc.):
        exercises, drill, memorization
-mythology (the heroes) and other Roman topics
        (architecture, government etc.)
-more etymology (new roots, suffixes, word formation in Latin)

8th grade: . . . . *Latin I* . . . . *Novice*
(or 7-8th grade:)
(or 6-7-8th grade:)

-listening, reading aloud
-reading simple stories
-learning basic forms and structures of Latin
-mythology, Roman stories
-etymology: roots & prefixes
-elements of English grammar and sentence structure

4th-5th grade: . . . . *Introduction to Latin* . . . . *Novice*
-songs, skits & games in Latin
-pronunciation of sounds of Latin
-simple roots and prefixes
-phonics (spelling)
-storytelling: myths and legends
-reading of simple sentences, dialogues & stories in Latin

B. Sample Syllabi

The purpose of the inclusion of these syllabi is to give an idea of the range of differences among Latin programs in the United States. We received syllabi from many teachers across the country and we are including the following as samples, not as guides. Each teacher's circumstances and situation is unique and each syllabus will reflect numerous factors that influence the amount of textbook material covered. Please note, in addition, that we have included information on textbooks only. Syllabus contributors included notes on the use of supplementary materials (especially the AMSCO review books), and on topics and units other than those in their textbooks. Thus, these syllabi represent only a part of the complete programs of the teachers who sent them to us. Also, some of these syllabi may have changed since this information was collected.

High School

Latin For Americans, Ullman et al.

Latin I . . . . Latin for Americans (1) . . . Units I-XI
Latin II . . . . Latin for Americans (2) . . . Units I-IV & Caesar readings

Julia Kolander,
Millard North High School, Omaha, Nebraska

———

Latin I . . . . Latin for Americans (1) . . . Units I-X
Latin II . . . . Latin for Americans (1) . . . Units XI-XIII
                      Latin for Americans (2) . . . Units I-VI
Latin III . . . . . . Latin for Americans (2) . . . Units VII-XI

Chad Dutcher,
Gaylord High School, Gaylord, Michigan

———

Our Latin Heritage, Hines

Latin I . . . . Our Latin Heritage . . . . . . Units 1-52
Latin II . . . . Our Latin Heritage . . . . . . to p. 254

A. Marino,
Howland High School, Warren, Ohio

———

Latin I . . . . Our Latin Heritage . . . . . . Units 1-32
Latin II . . . . Our Latin Heritage . . . . . . Units 33-40 & Gallic Wars (excerpts)

Kathy Elifrits,
Rolla High School, Rolla, Missouri

———

Cambridge Latin Course, NACCP

Latin I . . . . Cambridge Latin Course . . Units I and II & Beginning of Unit III
Latin II . . . . Cambridge Latin Course . . Units III and IV

Anne Shaw,
Lawrence High School, Lawrence, Kansas

———

Grade 7 . . . . Cambridge Latin Course . . Unit I
Grade 8 . . . . Cambridge Latin Course . . Units IIA & IIB
(Grade 9 and above: Units I & II & IIB)
Latin II . . . . Cambridge Latin Course . . Units III A & III B

Dobbie Nichols,
John Jay, Jr. H.S. & Sr. H.S., Katonah, NY

———

First Year Latin, Jenney et al.

Latin I . . . . First Year Latin . . . . Lessons 1-36
Latin II . . . . First Year Latin . . . . Lessons 36-60 & 150 pp. of 2nd Year Latin

Joan Sullivan,
Lincoln High School, Portland, OR

———

Latin I . . . . First Year Latin . . . . Lessons 1-44
Latin II . . . . Second Year Latin . . . . . . Lessons 1-12 & Jason, Ovid & Caesar

Patricia Keating,
Belmont High School, Belmont, MA

———

Latin I . . . . First Year Latin . . . . Lessons 1-28
Latin II . . . . First Year Latin . . . . Lessons 29-52

Kathy Elifrits,
Rolla High School, Rolla, Missouri

———

Latin I . . . . First Year Latin (1990 ed.) . Lessons 1-20
Latin II . . . . First Year Latin . . . . Lessons 21-40 w/ selected readings

Linda Sharrard Montross,
Madison High School, Vienna, VA

———

Ecce Romani Series, Longman

Latin I . . . . Ecce Romani . . . . Lessons 1-20

Latin II . . . . Ecce Romani . . . . Lessons 21-38
Latin III . . . . Ecce Romani . . . . Lessons 39-54 & Pliny
Princess Dillard,
Patrick Henry H.S., Richmond, VA

Latin I (grades 7 & 8) . . . . Ecce Romani 1-26
(or Latin I grade 9 and above) . . . . Ecce Romani 1-26
Latin II . . . . Ecce Romani . . . . . . 27- part of Book 4
Latin II . . . . finish book 4; Caesar & Cicero readings
Peggy Brucia, Nora Keith and Stephanie Stephans,
Port Jefferson Schools, Port Jefferson NY

Grade 6 . . . . Polsky, First Latin . . . . Chapters 1-27
Grade 7 . . . . Ecce Romani 1 . . . . Lessons 1-16
Grade 8 . . . . Ecce Romani 2 . . . . Lessons 17-26
Grade 9 . . . . Ecce Romani 3-4 . . . . Lessons 27-45
Helen Zanette,
Lynbrook North Middle School, Lynbrook, NY

Latin I . . . . Ecce Romani 1&2 . . . . . . Lessons 1-26
Latin II . . . . Ecce Romani 3&4 . . . . . . Lessons 27-53
Sally Davis,
Wakefield H.S. & H.B.Woodlawn Program, Arlington, VA

Mixed Textbooks
Latin I . . . . Jenney, First Year Latin 1-32
Latin II . . . . Jenney, First Year Latin (finish)
                      & Hines, Our Latin Heritage,
                      selected readings, incl. Caesar
Ann Bustard,
J.T.Barber H.S. & New Bern Sr. H.S., Craven County, NC

Latin I . . . . Jenney, First Year Latin . . . . 1-32+
Latin II . . . . Henle's Second Year Latin
                      & Caesar readings
P. Denning & D. Hoffman,
St. Ignatius College Prep., Chicago, IL

College Syllabi

	sem 1	sem 2	(sem 3)
Latin: An Introductory Course, Wheelock & *English Grammar for Latin Students*, Goldman & Szymanski & PLATO CAI Richard LaFleur, University of Georgia, Athens, GA	Chapters 1-15	16-30	
Latin: An Introductory Course, Wheelock & *38 Latin Stories*, Groton & May Sister Pauline Nugent, University of Texas, Austin, TX	Chapters 1-27	28-40	
Latin Via Ovid, Goldman & Nyenhuis & workbook: *Practice! Practice!* Stan Iverson, Concordia College, Moorhead, MN	Chapters 1-20	& *Fabulae Faciles*	
Latin Via Ovid , Goldman & Nyenhuis Mrs. J. Vanderbilt, Drury College, Springfield, MO	Chapters 1-18	finish book	
Reading Latin, Jones & Sidwell & Colby, *Grammar Review* & review Joseph O'Connor, Georgetown University, Washington, D.C.	Parts 1&2	Parts 3&4	Part 5
Cambridge Latin Course & workbooks (Units IVA &IVB: semester 4) University of Massachusetts at Amherst	Unit 1	Unit 2	Unit 3
Reading Latin, Ball John Ziolkowski, George Washington University, Washington, D.C.	Lessons 1-38	Lessons 39-76	

	sem 1	sem 2	(sem 3)
Latin For Reading, Knudsvig, Craig & Seligson John Siman, Catholic University, Washington, D.C.	Lessons 1-21	Lessons 22-35	
Latin For Reading Knudsvig, Craig & Seligson P. Cohee, B. Hill, C. Jenkinson, University of Colorado, Boulder, CO	Lessons 1-19	Lessons 18 - 35	
Traditio, P. Johnston (& *English Grammar for Latin Students,* Goldman & Szymanski) John Fisher, Wabash College, Crawfordsville, IL	Chap. 1- 11	review 1-11, finish bk.	
Traditio, P. Johnston Ken Kitchell, Louisiana State University, Baton Rouge, LA	Chap. 1-8	Chap. 9-17	
Ecce Romani, Longman Christine Brogan, University of Maryland, College Park, MD	Books 1&2	Books 3&4	
Oxford Latin Course, Balme & Morwood N. Rick Heatley, Washington & Lee University, Lexington, VA	Part 1	Part 2	Part 3

C. Enrollment Figure Tables

LATIN ENROLLMENTS, CLASSICAL ASSOCIATION MEMBERSHIPS, AND LATIN/GREEK EXAM PARTICIPANTS
1960–1990

Column groups: **Enrollments** (H.S. Latin[1] 9-12; College Latin[2]; College Greek[2] (Ancient)) — **Memberships** (NJCL, NSCL, ACL, APA, CAMWS Area[3], CAMWS Total[4], CAAS, CAPN, CANE, AIA, CAC) — **Natl. Latin Exam** — **Participants** (Latin AT, Latin AP, Natl. Greek Exam, Natl. Myth Exam)

Year	H.S. Latin[1] 9-12	College Latin[2]	College Greek[2] (Ancient)	NJCL	NSCL	ACL	APA	CAMWS Area[3]	CAMWS Total[4]	CAAS	CAPN	CANE	AIA	CAC	Natl. Latin Exam	Latin AT	Latin AP	Natl. Greek Exam	Natl. Myth Exam
1960	654,670	25,700[5]	12,700[5]	72,280		4622		2192	4363			892	2746			10,048	208		
1961	695,297			84,070		5497		2296	4577			930	3014			13,474	352		
1962	702,135			101,416		5613	1568	2378	4696			933	3404			16,980	439		
1963	680,234			105,238		5936	1685	2541	5027			929	3693			17,788	677		
1964	590,047			107,086		6252	1784	2591	5143			921	3868			20,244	862		
1965	591,445	39,600[6]	19,500[6]	101,810	213	6120	1855	2649	5184	950[5]		934	4202			22,297	885		
1966				106,990	448	6064	2053	2736	5239	953		954	4520			20,670	984		
1967				98,201	694	5855	2175	2698	5112	956		973	5173			19,561	882		
1968	371,977	34,981	17,516	88,727		5812	2355	2768	5244	860		906	5996	560		18,462	971		
1969				51,437	766	5209	2468	2682	5205	841		904	6446	518		15,920	1208		
1970	265,293	27,591	16,697	52,339		4465	2586	2606	4816			841	6753	582		12,777	1046		
1971				43,741	674	4118	2770	2600	4618			780	6867	580		7,460	975		
1972				39,772		3872	2765	2512	4449			730	6889	619		5,425	853		
1973				36,890		3444	2837	2231	3968			752	6695	636		4,231	705		
1974	167,165	25,167	24,391	32,918	610	3562	2861	1991	3524		124	724	6202	667		3,049	611		
1975				28,894		3469	2900	1916	3443		127	714	5752	547		1,433	624		
1976	150,470	24,403	25,843	30,532	632	2970	2928	1872	3535	750[5]	129	651	6063	562		1,555	745		
1977				28,870	543	2814		1834	3357	685	125	641	6999	554		1,734	841		
1978	151,782			29,010		2771	2864	1754	3100	787	132	576	7601	548	9,000[5]	1,725	880		
1979				31,152		2890	2855	1654	3071	734	122	616	7923	542	16,497	1,649	1016		
1980		25,035	22,111	32,026	600	2880	2847	1618	2915		141	606	8758	559	20,710	2,060	1122		
1981				33,924		3006	2932	1657	2881		120	645	9680	557	27,602	2,258	1261	310	
1982	169,580			37,017	659	2995	3025	1575	2753		109	662	8981	559	33,336	2,587	1311	415	
1983		24,224	19,350	40,574	643	2980	3087	1611	2757	643	107	712	8717	548	35,604	2,455	1529	597	
1984				44,452	550	3061	3093	1651	2805	630	99	756	8645	535	46,565	2,685	1704	545	
1985				48,350	525[5]	3088		1613	2682	682	120	777	8739	533	53,505	2,865	1929	639	
1986	176,841	25,038	17,608	49,489	478	3472	2890	1637	2809	675	106	810	8668		60,026	3,140	2104	752	
1987				46,902	485	3649	2925	1669	2865	781	124		7545		60,758	3,227	2545	957	
1988				48,416	562	3626	2970	1646	2707	656	132		7230		63,750	3,617	2630	813	
1989				51,320	522	3896	3018	1623	2741	652	128		7560		69,205	3,452	2688	779	
1990				52,562	534	3844	2966	1657	2711	678	135		8505		71,457	3,338	2712	795	3208

Abbreviations: NJCL, National Junior Classical League; NSCL, National Senior Classical League; ACL, American Classical League; APA, American Philological Association; CAMWS, Classical Association of the Middle West and South; CAAS, Classical Association of the Atlantic States; CAPN, Classical Association of the Pacific Northwest; CANE, Classical Association of New England; AIA, Archaeological Institute of America; CAC, Classical Association of Canada; Latin AT, the College Board's Latin Achievement Test; Latin AP, the College Board's Latin Advanced Placement Exam.

[1]Source: ACTFL. [2]Source: MLA. [3]Includes only members in the thirty CAMWS states and two Canadian provinces. [4]Includes, in addition to CAMWS area members, subscribers to the *Classical Journal* (the association's journal) from outside CAMWS territory. [5]Estimated. [6]Rounded to the nearest hundred by MLA.

Table updated from R.A. LaFleur, ed., *The Teaching of Latin in American Schools: A Profession in Crisis* (Atlanta, GA: Scholars Press, 1987; 1989 rpt. available from ACL, Miami University, Oxford, OH 45056)

Selected Bibliography
& Some Useful Addresses

SELECTED BIBLIOGRAPHY

Introduction

Advisory Committee of the ACL. *The Classical Investigation, Part One: General Report* (Princeton, NJ: Princeton University Press, 1924).

Burns, Mary Ann T. & O'Connor, Joseph F. *The Classics in American Schools: Teaching the Ancient World* (Atlanta: Scholars Press 1987). Available @ $5.50 from Professor Ed Phinney, Department of Classics, University of Massachusetts, Amherst, MA 01003. Make checks payable to "APA."

Kennedy, George A., "The History of Latin Education," *Helios*, 14.2 (Fall 1987) 7-16.

Phinney, Ed, "The Current Classical Scene in America," *J.A.C.T. Review*, Second Series, No. 2 (Autumn 1987) 2-7. Reprinted in *The Classical Outlook*, 66 (May-June 1989) 117-25.

Reinhold, Meyer, "The Latin Tradition in the United States," *Helios*, 14.2 (Fall 1987) 123-139.

Elementary/Middle-School Latin

Baca, Albert R. et al., "Language Transfer Project of the Los Angeles Unified School District," *The Classical Outlook*, 56 (1979) 74-80.

Masciantonio, Rudolph, "Tangible Benefits of the Study of Latin: A Review of the Research," *Foreign Language Annals*, 10 (1977) 375-82.

Mavrogenes, Nancy, "Latin and the Language Arts: An Update," *Foreign Language Annals*, 20 (1987) 131-37. Reprinted in *The Classical Outlook*, 66 (1989) 78-83.

Polsky, Marion, "The NEH/Brooklyn College Latin Cornerstone Project, 1982-84: Genesis, Implementation, Evaluation," *The Classical Outlook*, 63 (1986) 77-83.

High School Latin

LaFleur, Richard A., "The Study of Latin in American Schools: Success and Crisis," in R. A. LaFleur, ed. *The Teaching of Latin in American Schools: A Profession in Crisis* (Atlanta: Scholars' Press 1987).

Latimer, John F. *The Oxford Conference and Related Activities: A Report to the National Endowment for the Humanities* (Oxford, OH: ACL, 1968).

Lawall, G. *ACTFL Selected Listing of Instructional Materials for Elementary and Secondary School Programs: Latin and Greek* (Yonkers, NY: ACTFL, 1988).

National Latin Exam Committee, "The National Latin Exam: 1978-85," *The Classical Outlook*, 62 (1984-85) 45-47.

"Outcomes for Classical Languages," in *Academic Preparation in Foreign Language: Teaching for Transition from High School to College* (NY: College Entrance Examination Board, 1986), pp. 26-28.

Santirocco, Matthew S., ed. *Latinitas: The Tradition and Teaching of Latin*. A Special Issue of *Helios*, 14.2 (Lubbock, TX: Texas Tech University, 1987).

Strasheim, Lorraine A., "Latin in the 1990's and Beyond," *NASSP Curriculum Report*, 20 (1990) 1-4.

College and University Latin & Classics

Moreland, Floyd L. *Strategies in Teaching Greek and Latin: Two Decades of Experimentation* (Chico, CA: Scholars Press, 1981).

Morford, Mark, "Teaching Courses in Greek and Roman Civilizations and Classical Mythology," in Douglas M. Astolfi, ed. *Teaching the Ancient World* (Chico, CA: Scholars Press, 1983), p. 151-83.

Teacher Education

Davis, Sally; Daugherty, Gregory; Larrick, David; Mikalson, Jon; and Miller, John, "Preparation and Training for Teachers of Latin," *Classical Journal*, 86.3 (February–March 1991) 262–267.

Keitel, Elizabeth, "A Model for Latin Teacher Training: The MAT Program at the University of Massachusetts, " in R. A. LaFleur, ed. *The Teaching of Latin in American Schools: A Profession in Crisis* (Atlanta: Scholars Press, 1987), pp. 63-70.

SOME USEFUL ADDRESSES

American Classical League (ACL) (TMRC)
Miami University
Oxford, OH 45056

ACL/NJCL National Latin Exam (NLE)
P. O. Box 95
Mt. Vernon, VA 22121

ACL/NJCL National Greek Examination (NGE)
Ed Phinney, Chair
Department of Classics
University of Massachusetts
Amherst, MA 01003

American Council of Teachers
of Foreign Language (ACTFL)
6 Executive Plaza
Yonkers, NY 10703-6801

American Philological Association (APA)
Department of Classics
College of the Holy Cross
Worcester, MA 01610-2395

Advanced Placement Program (CEEB/ETS)
Princeton, NJ 08541

Association of Departments of
Foreign Languages (ADFL)
(subsidiary of the Modern Language Assoc.)
10 Astor Place
New York, N.Y. 10003

Classics Chronicle
8951 S.W. 10 Terrace
Miami, FL 33174

Elementary Teachers of Classics (ETC)
c/o American Classical League
Miami University
Oxford, OH 45056

JCCAE (ACL-APA Joint Committee on the
Classics in American Education)
Ed Phinney, Chair
Department of Classics
University of Massachusetts
Amherst, MA 01003

Iuvenis & *Adulescens*
Midwest European Publications, Inc.
915 Foster Street
Evanston, IL 60201

Omnibus
Joint Association of Classical Teachers (JACT)
Ed Phinney, American Representative, JACT
Department of Classics
University of Massachusetts
Amherst, MA 01003

National Committee for Latin and Greek (NCLG)
Virginia Barrett, Chair
6669 Vinahaven
Cypress, CA 90630

National Endowment for the Humanities (NEH)
1100 Pennsylvania Avenue, NW
Washington, D.C. 20506

National Junior Classical League (NJCL)
c/o American Classical League
Miami University
Oxford, OH 45056

Pompeiana, Inc.
6026 Indianola Ave.
Indianapolis, IN 46220

Vergilian Society of America
Robert Rowland, Executive Secretary
Classics Department
University of Maryland
College Park, MD 20742